East and West

Religions and Laws

Best regards
G. Popovici

Galina Popovici

ISBN: 9781073688036
Copyright © 2019 Galina Popovici
All rights reserved.
Library of Congress Control Number:2019910264

Editor Diane Peterson

This is a rewritten and supplemented author translation
from Russian language of the book "Восток и Запад.
Вера, Религии и Законы"

(ISBN-10:1541208285, ISBN-13:978-1541208285)

Another book of the author
Milestones of Russian history.
Past and possible future of Russia.
ISBN -13: 978-1546360315
ISBN-10: 154636031X

The fact is that the significance of peoples in the human race is determined only by their spiritual power and that the interest they arouse to themselves depends on their moral influence in the world, and not on the noise produced by them.

Peter Chaadaev

Real faith is not to know which days are lean, in which ones to go to the temple and in which to listen to and read prayers, but to always live a good life in love with everyone, always deal with your neighbors as you wish to come with you.

Leo Tolstoy

Not to resist evil does not mean not to fight against evil: on the contrary, it means to fight evil, but not to fight a person, fight only against what is evil, wrong in a person, fight evil, compassionate and loving a person possessed by evil.

Leo Tolstoy

To Astrid, Ann and Alina

CONTENTS

Introduction

Part I

Pre-Christian religions

Part II

Christianity

INTRODUCTION

At some level of development, people began to ask how the world works and how to live. They tried to explain why there is day and night, winter and summer, why there are storms, droughts, fires, floods, or what happens to a person after his death. Religions tried to answer these questions. Answers have changed with the development and transformation of society.

At first, people believed that the world was inhabited by invisible spirits, elements of nature deities and souls of deceased ancestors, supernatural beings, good and evil. It was believed that they are actively involved in people's lives. These first beliefs were called pagan or folk.

With the evolution of mankind, religions appeared that were based on a common belief in one God or a group of gods. As a rule, religions provided for participation in prayer and rituals, and often contained a moral code regulating human behavior.

At the beginning, when people lived in tribes, there was

no need for laws, since all relationships, like in the family, were determined by feelings of love, hatred, or jealousy.

The word civilization is derived from the Latin word *civitas* — city, and *civis* — a resident of the city. When people began to live in cities and united into states, there was a need to order their relations between themselves and the state, i.e. create a code of laws. To be a civilized person is to abide the laws.

Historically, codes of law were formulated on the basis of moral teachings of religions. The laws of society — civil laws — usually apply for a period of time. They change with the development and transformation of society.

At first, some religions had two tasks: they explained the material structure of the world and answered the question of how to live. But already in the middle of the first millennium BCE, Eastern religions appeared: Taoism, Confucianism, Buddhism, which answered the question of how to live and gave no explanation for the appearance and structure of the world. It was believed that the world always existed. In these religions, believers worship their teachers — Lao Tzu, Confucius, and Buddha.

Over time, the theme of the material organization of the world turned to science. But the answer to the question of how to live has remained for religions. In the sixteenth century Nicolaus Copernicus showed that the Earth is not the center of the universe. Scientists have found that the creation of the world given in the Old Testament is wrong. Many atheists appeared among the educated people. Together with the scientific mistakes of the Christian religion, atheists automatically rejected the achievements of religion in the moral field. They threw out the baby with the bathwater.

Religions define culture as a lifestyle built by a group of people and passed on from one generation to another. Culture tells people how to behave in one or another occasion, and usually this behavior is determined by the prevailing religion of a given society.

I will give a few examples.

In Buddhism, it is believed that life is suffering, so you should rejoice at the death of any individual, even the closest one, because he was freed of suffering. Of course, a person can be hurt if someone close to him died, but he should not show his grief.

I will tell one case from Thailand, a Buddhist country. The man died. He was 82 years old. He was laid in the monastery hall, in an open coffin for 3 days, during which people came to show respect to him. When we entered, his joyful, smiling sister greeted us and behaved as if we were at a birthday party, not at a funeral. Everyone smiled and rejoiced.

The opposite attitude to death is in the Christian culture, where a person's life is considered the highest good. If a loved one dies, you don't have to hide your pain.

Another case. In some Arab countries, Islam prohibits women from driving a car, going outside without being accompanied by their husbands, obliges them to wear the burqa. Girls are brought up in the belief that such a life is the right and only possible one.

Once I talked with a female student from an Arab country. I told her that she was trying to get a diploma that she would not need in her country, since she would not be able to work or even drive a car. She replied that she was studying not for her diploma, but for her development. In her country, she will marry and take care of her husband and children, live a happy, she hopes, family life. The student said that she is very sorry for American women whose lives are spent in work and stress: 8 hours of work, where a woman should strive to be the best or at least a good worker, otherwise they will take someone else; the road with its peak hours, where people often lose time and nerves, and then they hurry to kindergartens or schools to pick up children. The life of American women is a constant stress. The student said she would not want such a life. I must note that Arab students studying in America come from rich or at least well-off families. I do not know how a woman from a less prosperous social class would answer my question.

Another student told me that her husband can take a

second wife, when they return home, because men are now allowed to have four wives. That was the greatest fear of her life.

Anyone who has been abroad can cite many such examples.

Even atheists have to admit that they live according to Christian culture if they live in countries where the Christian church is predominant.

This book examines the relationship and interdependence of religion and laws, their history and their influence on the fate of humanity, the influence of religions on the culture and history of the East and the West.

Part I

PRE-CHRISTIAN
RELIGIONS

1. PAGANISM

Paganism is a huge complex of primitive beliefs and rituals that developed in ancient times. The first beliefs of the people were primitive. Pagans believed in spirits: water, wood goblins, house spirits, and the like, generally in supernatural or otherworldly forces, which, they thought, control the people's lives.

Paganism survived to modern times in remote regions where civilization has not reached, where people live in tribes and have little education. For example, in Thailand, 95% of the population are Buddhists, and 5% are pagan tribes living in the mountains. In the university park in Thailand, I saw two students who served food and drinks on a table under a decorated tree. The girls told me that they bring food to the spirits that live in the trees. Although the girls were students, they kept the faith of their families living in the mountains.

Similar decorated trees I were seen near Lake Baikal in

Russia. These trees were decorated by the Buryats. But my Russian friends who had a higher education also hung their ribbons on these trees making a wish. Just in case, it might come true. A remarkable study of Russian beliefs, superstitions, and prejudices was done by Vladimir Dal [1]. Beliefs, superstitions and prejudices, about which Dal writes, are widespread in Russia to this day. Little has changed in the century and a half since the Dal's publication.

The story about the Peruvian Indians was told to me by an English woman (let's call her Mary) who worked under the guidance of the World Health Organization in Peru 30 years ago. She worked there for nine years among the tribes who lived high in the mountains. The government never reached those places, and people lived there just as they lived for thousands of years. Mary worked there as a medical assistant, pharmacist, and midwife. She lived in a settlement with Catholic missionaries who made roads and built a school where they taught.

The tribes of Peruvian Indians were pagans. They believed in the forces of nature: mountains, lakes, rivers, wind, rain, thunderstorms. People lived with constant superstitious fears. In the mountains, a person had to pray before starting to climb or to descend. They had to pray before entering the water of a lake or river. Mary told the case of one man who entered the lake without a prayer, slipped, fell, then came home, lay down and did not get up until he died. He had no physical injury. He was sure that the lake punished him, and he must die.

Mary told about the laws by which the tribes lived. The basic law was "an eye for an eye, a tooth for a tooth, a life for a life." The leader of the tribe had to follow the observance of the laws, but he was not always wise enough, strong enough, and sometimes simply indifferent, and thus the resolution of problems lay on the participants themselves. As a result, these laws gave an advantage to the strong. If a strong one knocked out a tooth to weak one and a weak one tried to respond in the same way, a strong one could knock several more teeth from him. The law "life for life" obliged the family of the murdered man to kill someone from the killer's family - blood feud. But if the families were equally strong, then the revenge could continue through many generations.

Life in these tribes was worth nothing. Family planning was carried out by killing newborns, especially girls. They did not know means of protection from pregnancy, or abortion. After the birth, unwanted babies were killed. This society was not able to protect the weak.

2. SUMER CIVILIZATION

Sumer civilization was one of the oldest civilizations which, along with the Egyptian civilization, had the strongest influence on all subsequent civilizations [1-2]. Civilization existed from 4500 BCE until 1750 BCE in the southern part of Mesopotamia on the territory of modern Iraq.

For about two thousand five hundred years of its existence, the Sumerians invented writing, bronze, metal processing, a wheel and a potter's wheel. We still enjoy the fruits of their successes in astronomy and mathematics. The Sumerians divided the year into four seasons, twelve months. They measured angles, minutes and seconds in six dozen - as their calculus was based on 10 and 60. They knew how to burn brick and build multi-story palaces and cities out of it.

The Sumerians were polytheists. Each city of Sumer had its patron god. Elaborate polity protected the rights of every

Sumer - they had a jury and democratically elected governing bodies.

The codes of laws that have come down to us is the laws of the Sumerians.

The very first code of laws - the Code of King Ur-Nammu - was compiled in approximately 2100-2050 BC [3].

"Ur-Nammu with its own laws" established justice in the country, eradicating disorder and lawlessness." He ensured that "an orphan does not become a victim of a rich man; a widow is a victim of a strong one." This is what the introduction to the code says, from which only five articles were possible to read.

Here are three of them:

"If [man to man by tool] hurt his arm or leg, 10 shekels of silver he must pay" (§ 16).

"If a man broke a bone to a man ... 1 mine of silver, he must pay" (§ 17).

"If a person damaged the face of a person with a tool 2/3 of the mine

silver he must pay "(§ 18)."

The Code of King Hammurabi, which reached us in the form of a cuneiform inscription on a black diorite stele, was compiled later, after three and a half centuries (1750 BC).

At the top of the pillar is Hammurabi, who receives the laws from the hands of the Sun God sitting on the throne. Notice that the fair laws were given to Hammurabi by God, that is, God taught people how to live correctly.

Part of the text of the laws was shot down and partially restored by quotations of laws on clay tablets. The focus of the laws was economic, household and family relations. In Mesopotamia, the "presumption of innocence" was observed (innocent until proven otherwise).

The introduction says that the Gods handed Hammurabi royal power to protect the weak, orphans and widows from insults and oppression from the strong. This is followed by 282 articles of laws. Some of the laws of Hammurabi are very briefly listed on Wikipedia. A full list of laws is given on this site [4].

I cite only a few laws:

1-4: protection of the honor and dignity of citizens. The punishment is very strong - "If a person accused another person and blamed him for the murder, but did not prove it, the accuser must be killed."

8: if a person steals either an ox, or a sheep, or a donkey, or a pig, or a boat, then if it belongs to a god or a palace, he must pay a thirtyfold amount, and if it belongs to a mushkenum (ordinary citizen), he must compensate tenfold. If the thief has nothing to pay, he must be killed

14: Abduction of children: the punishment is death

21: Inviolability of the home of citizens: the punishment is death.

22-24: compensation for damage caused to a person by

robbers - the community or the headman had to pay for all the damage.

25: Theft in case of fire - punishment: "a person must be thrown into this fire".

The warriors received land plots from the state, which were inherited through the male line and were inalienable. The warrior was obliged at the first request of the king to make a campaign.

The afterword says: "These are the just laws that Hammurabi set up, the mighty king, thereby giving the country true happiness and good governance.

I am Hammurabi, the king, perfect ... I was not careless ... I eradicated civil strife, improved the situation of the country, settled people in safe places and saved them from fear. The great gods called me, and therefore I am a shepherd peacemaker, whose scepter is straight. My good canopy is spread over my city, and I hold on my bosom the people of the country of Sumer and Akkad. With the help of my patron goddess, they began to prosper, I led them to well-being and covered them with my wisdom. So that the strong do not oppress the weak, to render justice to an orphan and a widow, in Babylon ... to judge the court of the country, render decisions of the country and the oppressed to give justice, I wrote my precious words on my monument and installed it before effigy of me, king of justice.

3. CIVILIZATION OF ANCIENT EGYPT

Egypt is the oldest and longest-lived civilization (approximately four thousand years), which had a tremendous impact on the beliefs and culture of modern Western civilization. The cosmology and religion of Egypt are at the core of the religion of Judaism.

The first written myths of Egypt that have come down to us date back to about 25th century BC, although the oral transmission of myths could have been earlier.

The god of Atum (Aten, Amon) was considered the creator of the world - the original source of everything that exists, finished, perfect, absolute. He created himself from nothing, created the world from the original ocean of chaos and established order in the whole universe. He created Maat - truth, justice, universal harmony, divine institution and ethical standard.

The Egyptians believed that Atum is in all elements of the world. He is also the forefather of all gods. The first were created god of air Shu and goddess Tefnut (moisture, dew, rain). Their children were Geb (earth) and Nut (sky), and grandchildren — Osiris (death and rebirth), Isis (marriage, motherhood, health), Seth (desert, storm, war, unrest), Seth's wife Neftis (death and mourning). This was followed by grandchildren, great-grandchildren, and so on - many gods and goddesses of general Egyptian and local significance. The Egyptians believed that gods govern all the phenomena of nature and the fate of people.

Throughout history, the names of the gods and their functions sometimes changed. One of the most revered gods was the sun god Ra. Later there was the unification of the creator god - Amon and the god Ra: Amon-Ra.

The Egyptians, like the Sumerians, had its own patron god for each city. In Egypt, there was also a period of monotheism during the New Kingdom, when Pharaoh Akhenaten (1353–1336 BC) abolished the official cult of other gods in favor of the god of creators Aten. The exclusion of all but one God was a radical departure from the Egyptian tradition. After the death of Akhenaten, the Egyptians returned to their local gods, whom they had worshiped for centuries.

The Egyptians believed in the immortality of the soul. Temples and tombs had painted scenes of eternal afterlife. The soul of the dead had to account for their deeds on earth. The trial of the dead, according to the "Book of the Dead"

[1], was as follows: The deceased was judged by "Weighing the Heart". The deceased swore that he had not committed any sin from the list of Maat 42 principles. The heart of the deceased was aggravated by his sins. Then the heart was weighed on a scale, comparing the weight of the deceased with the weight of the goddess Maat, who embodied the truth, justice and ethical standards.

If the scales were balanced, it meant that the deceased led a decent life. Sinners who did not comply with the moral requirements of the questions were devoured by the monster [2].

The soul of the righteous, who answered all questions correctly, went to the kingdom of the dead in her earthly body. Since the soul used its original body, the Egyptians embalmed the dead, and Pharaoh and the rich Egyptians built pyramids to preserve the body of the deceased as long as possible.

Below - 42 principles of Maat, 42 negative confessions, that is, answers to questions posed by the gods.

1. I did not commit sin.
2. I did not commit robbery with violence.
3. I did not steal.
4. I did not kill men and women.
5. I did not steal the grain.
6. I did not steal the offerings.
7. I did not steal the property of God.

8. I did not utter a lie.

9. I was not into food.

10. I did not utter a curse.

11. I did not commit adultery.

12. I have not slept with men.

13. I didn't make anyone cry.

14. I have not eaten my heart [that is, I was not upset, or useless, or did not feel remorse].

15. I did not attack any person.

16. I am not a man of deception.

17. I did not steal from cultivated land.

18. I was not a spy.

19. I did not slander a person.

20. I was not angry without good reason.

21. I did not corrupt the wife of any man.

22. I did not pollute myself.

23. I did not terrorize.

24. I have not transgressed [the Law].

25. I was not angry.

26. I have not closed my ears to the words of truth.

27. I did not blame.

28. I am not a man of violence.

29. I did not sow hostility (or outraged calm).

30. I did not act (or tried) with excessive haste.

31. I did not get into questions.

32. I did not multiply my words in conversation.

33. I have not offended anyone; I have not done evil.
34. I did not work in witchcraft against the king (or blasphemy against the king).
35. I have never stopped [the streams] of water.
36. I never raised my voice (spoke arrogantly, or in anger).
37. I did not curse (or blaspheme) God.
38. I did not speak with arrogance.
39. I did not steal the bread of the gods.
40. I did not take Kenfu's cakes from the spirits of the dead.
41. I did not snatch the bread from the child, and do not treat with contempt the God of my city.
42. I did not kill the cattle belonging to God.

The most remarkable thing in the Egyptian religion was the equality of all before the gods. Pharaoh, who was considered the messenger of the gods, had to report after death for his deeds, just like a mere mortal.

The basis of relationships in Egyptian society was morality. Egypt usually did not attack other countries (principles - do not kill or order to kill), but always maintained an army since it had to defend itself against the attack of various nomads. Throughout history the borders of Egypt have changed little. During Ramses II there was a long war between the Hittites (the people of Asia Minor), who constantly attacked Egypt, and the Egyptians. Ramses, defeating the Hittites, did not annex their territory to Egypt, but concluded a peace treaty with them, the first in world history, and thus ended the war. Egypt has never been a world empire, like Persia or Rome, although for many centuries it was the most developed and powerful nation in the world.

4. JUDAISM

Moses, the founder of Judaism (presumably the twelfth to thirteenth century BCE), was, according to the Bible, a prophet. a religious leader, and legislator. To Moses is attributed the authorship of the Torah, the first five books of the Old Testament, the Holy Scriptures of Judaism. Moses is also an important prophet in Christianity, Islam, and other denominations.

As the adopted son of the Egyptian princess, Moses was a highly educated person. The maturity of Moses could coincide with the rule of Pharaoh Akhenaten, the monotheist. Moses preached the existence of one God for his nation - Yahweh (Jehovah), as did Pharaoh Akhenaten - for the Egyptians.

According to Genesis One, the first chapter of the Bible the grandson of Abraham, Jacob, and his sons migrated to Egypt during a seven-year drought and famine in their land, Canaan. At this time in the prosperous Egypt the youngest son of Jacob, Joseph, held an important position at the court of Pharaoh. Jews in Egypt were slaves, lived there for 300 - 400 years. At the behest of the Jewish God Yahweh, Moses led the Jews from Egypt to Israel, the land promised by Yahweh to the Jews. A vow was made between Yahweh and the Jews - Jews will worship only their God Yahweh and no other Gods. Yahweh revealed the ten commandments to Moses. ("Exodus," second chapter of the Bible).

Sometimes the principles of Maat are written as commandments, that is, not as the answer of the dead to the gods, but as an order of the Gods. (Do not do evil, do not steal from your neighbor, etc.) Comparison of the commandments of Maat with the commandments of Moses is given in the book of Ernst Badge [1].

The 10 Commandments (Exodus, 20):

(1) You shall have no other gods ...

(2) Do not make yourself an idol ...

(3) Do not pronounce the name of the Lord, your God, in vain, ...

(4) Remember the Sabbath day, to keep it holy; ...

(5) Honor thy father and thy mother, ...

(6) Do not kill.

(7) Do not commit adultery.

(8) Do not steal.

(9) Do not give false testimony to your neighbor.

(10) Do not desire your neighbor's house ...

The first 3 commandments relate to the vow given by the Jews to the God Yahweh.

4th commandment: *Remember the Sabbath day by keeping it holy. [9] Six days you shall labor and do all your work, [10] but the seventh day is a sabbath to the LORD your God. On it you shall not do any work, neither you, nor your son or daughter, nor your male or female servant, nor your animals, nor any foreigner residing in your towns. [11] For in six days the LORD made the heavens and the earth, the sea, and all that is in them, but he rested on the seventh day. Therefore, the LORD blessed the Sabbath day and made it holy.* (Exodus 20: 8-11).

On the fourth commandment stays: *the Sabbath to the Lord your God: do not do any work in it, neither you, nor your son, nor your daughter, nor your slave, nor your animal* ... I think there is a question of work, as a vital provision, i.e. work, giving a livelihood. In European languages, domestic affairs are usually called "household chores, housekeeping, etc." Usually they are not equated to work as means of subsistence. Therefore, the application of this commandment in everyday life may have different interpretations. One of them is the global interpretation that people go to work for 6 (now 5) days, and on the rest of 1 or 2 days they solve their personal problems that are not related to their work. The second interpretation is the interpretation of the Israeli radicals, that a person should not do anything at all on Saturday. I give a few examples, which look strange at least. The believer does not have to talk on the phone, because he has to pick up the phone. In hotels there is an elevator that stops on all floors, in order not to press the button of the desired floor. But a believer still does some work, for example, he dresses, washes his hands, eats, etc.

In chapters 21-23 of the Exodus, 99 laws are given by which the Jews must live.

In chapters 25-31, 34-40 the rules of religious rites are given.

The book of Leviticus contains 247 of 613 laws and rules of the Jewish religion. The book of Leviticus is devoted to the religious and cult side of the life of Israel, especially the sacrificial system. The content of the book forms a detailed development and direct continuation of the articles and resolutions of the law set forth in the second part of the book Exodus, the "Revelation, announced from Sinai."

The book "Numbers" describes 40 years of the journey of the Jewish people in the desert.

The last fifth Moses book "Deuteronomy" consists of 34 chapters. In this book, in addition to the 10 commandments, the laws of religious ceremonies, laws in relation to officials, civil and criminal laws are given. In addition, given the rules that must be respected in everyday life, for example, believers diet. It is indicated which animals, birds, fish you can eat, and which cannot, and so on. Many times, Moses in this book repeats the instructions to people to live by the laws:

8: 1 *Try to keep all the commandments I command you today, so that you may live and multiply ...*

8: 2 *Remember how the LORD your God led you all the way in the wilderness these forty years, to humble and test you in order to know what was in your heart, whether or not you would keep his commands.*

8: 3 *He humbled you, tormented you with hunger, and fed you with manna, which you did not know and your fathers did not know, in order to show you that man lives not with bread alone, but with every word that proceeds from the mouth of the Lord.*

Thus, Moses not only brought the Jews out of slavery, but also gave them a total of 613 commandments, laws and regulations relating to all aspects of life, including law, family, diet and hygiene. In the laws given by Moses, there is much life understanding and justice; Let me give you just one example - about the ruler of Israel (Deuteronomy 17:15-20).

[15] *be sure to appoint over you a king the LORD your God chooses. He must be from among your fellow Israelites. Do not place a foreigner over you, one who is not an Israelite.* [16] *The king, moreover, must not acquire great numbers of horses for himself or make the people return to*

Egypt to get more of them, for the LORD *has told you, "You are not to go back that way again." [17] He must not take many wives, or his heart will be led astray. He must not accumulate large amounts of silver and gold.*

[18] When he takes the throne of his kingdom, he is to write for himself on a scroll a copy of this law, taken from that of the Levitical priests. [19] It is to be with him, and he is to read it all the days of his life so that he may learn to revere the LORD *his God and follow carefully all the words of this law and these decrees [20] and not consider himself better than his fellow Israelites and turn from the law to the right or to the left. Then he and his descendants will reign a long time over his kingdom in Israel.*

Moses did not promise the Jews an eternal afterlife. He said that by fulfilling the laws they would be alive and multiply.

Moses wrote only five books of the Old Testament. During the millennium after Moses, the Old Testament was replenished with another 34 chapters containing history, prophecies, and poetry.

The Jews lived on the land promised by their god Yahweh and after about a thousand years gave to the world Jesus Christ, the Messiah, whose arrival the Bible predicted many times.

In the Bible there are strange, to say the least, stories that are incomprehensible to the modern reader. But there are also many great narrations. I will give a few examples: Psalms, the Song of Solomon - an unsurpassed love poem, Ecclesiastes' sad reflections, and many others. I give, as an example, a summary of the story of the righteous seeker Job.

Book of Job

One of the most impressive parables about the need to comply with the laws at all levels is the Book of Job from the Old Testament. The book is written in poetic language and is easy to read.

One day, heavenly beings came to God. Among them was Satan. Satan told God that he had walked the whole earth. God asked if he saw Job. God said that Job *is blameless, just, God-fearing and removed from evil.* Then Satan said: *Was Job God-fearing for nothing? Did you not protect him, and his house, and all that he has? You blessed the cause of his hands. But put your hand and touch all that he has - Does he bless you?* Then God allowed Satan to take everything that Job had, but not to touch Job himself. Satan took away the flock from Job, Job's children died, but Job didn't say anything bad about God. When God asked again about Job, Satan said: *... for the life of his man he will give everything he has. But put forth your hand and touch the bone of his, his flesh. Will he bless you?* God answered: *save thy soul, save thy hand.* Satan struck Job with fierce leprosy. Job's wife asked him: *You are still firm in your integrity! Then blaspheme God and die.*

Friends came to Job. They also demanded that Job repent of his sins, because if God punished Job, then it is clear that Job is guilty.

But Job does not agree. Job says he is blameless (chap. 29, 30) and demands a fair trial (chapters 13, 31). *Let them weigh in the balance of truth, and God will know my integrity* (31: 5). In addition, Job criticizes the order established by God (Chapter 21), when *the wicked live and reach old age* (21: 7). *Their houses are safe from fear, and there is no rod of God upon them* (21: 9). *So, listen to me, wise men! God cannot be wrong or the Almighty unjust* (34:10) So Job demanded from God the judgment for himself and the observance of the laws.

And God acknowledged that Job's criticism was correct. *And the Lord brought back the loss of Job ... and the Lord gave Job twice as much as he had before* (42:10). *And God blessed the last days of Job more than the former* (42:12) *After this, Job lived one hundred and forty years, and saw his sons and his son's sons to the fourth generation* (42:16)

Job was one of the first dissidents, we would say in modern language.

5. EAST ASIA RELIGIONS

The middle of the first millennium BCA was the period of the emergence of several religions in Asia. They brought a new vision of the world, different from older religions. Taoism, Confucianism, Buddhism became the great multi-million religions. These religions are moral teachings that show the road that a person must follow in order to live in peace and understanding with the people around him.

Taoism

Main Goal - Peace and Mental Well-Being
Who takes - fills the palms, who gives - fills the heart

The philosopher Lao Tzu (6th century BCA) is at the origin of the religion of Taoism. Lao Tzu was born in 604 BC. He was a highly educated man. For most of his life, he served as the custodian of the imperial archive and librarian in the state library during the Zhou dynasty. Lao Tzu wrote the text of the Tao Te Ching (Canon of the Way and its Good Power), the canonical book of Taoism [1].

Taoism embodies Tao, which means the path or way of life in harmony with the environment and yourself - completely authentic, sincere, natural and innocent. This is a life of balance.

The symbol of Taoism is called "Tai Ji", which means "the highest". It represents a circle that is divided into two parts. The white side is called Yin, and the dark side is called Yang. Small circles suggest that each half has a "seed" in the other half. The image represents the duality of all phenomena - active and passive principle, man and woman, life and death. For Taoists, Yin and Yang are not opposites. In fact, each of them must exist with the other and cannot exist without the presence of the other. The influence of human civilization is thought to upset the balance of Yin and Yang.

The symbol of Taoism is a deep idea of dialectics, which asserts that there is nothing absolute in life. There is no absolute Yin, and there is no absolute Yang. There is no separate life and death. There is always death in life and vice versa.

This idea of constant change, the coexistence and struggle of opposites was developed by the Greek philosopher Heraclitus, who lived in the sixth century BCE and could be a contemporary of Lao Tzu. Heraclitus argued that "if there was not a constant conflict of opposites, there would be no change of day and night, heat and cold, summer and winter, even life and death. Indeed, if some things did not die, others would not be born. The conflict does not hinder life, but rather is a prerequisite of life" [2]. In the nineteenth century, the idea of the development and struggle of opposites was investigated by the German philosopher Hegel.

Wu Wei is a state of inaction or balance, not a deed. The one who understands and adheres to Wu Wei should not try to force events, since the Universe is already working smoothly in accordance with its own laws, and human actions can disrupt the existing harmony. The path can only be found in humility, in the calm acceptance of life and things as they are, and in seeking understanding of the passage of time and the development of nature instead of creating situations according to your desires. Taoism, as a moral doctrine, has become one of the main religions of China.

An interesting aspect of Taoism is that it does not claim to be "divine inspiration." Lao Tzu never claimed that deities visited him and told him to write the Tao Te Ching.

Sayings, quotes and aphorisms of Lao Tzu can be found on the site [1]. I cite a few of them:

• When laws and orders multiply, the number of thieves and brigands grows.

• He who, knowing the limits of his activity, does not come close to dangers, will live a long time.

• He who, knowing nothing, behaves like a knower of everything, is sick.

• There are four great spheres: The Path, the Sky, the Earth, the Man - and the Man takes first place among the spheres.

• The law of the worthy is to do good and not to quarrel.

• The one who knows the measure is satisfied with his position. He who knows a lot is silent, and the one who speaks does not know much.

• The trouble of the whole world comes from trifles, as a great thing - from small things.

• Be able to know the beginning and the path of antiquity, and this knowledge will allow you to see the clue that leads to today.

• Be mindful of your thoughts - they are the beginning of actions.

• Everything in the world grows, blooms and returns to its root. Returning to your root means tranquility; consonant with nature means eternal; therefore, the destruction of the body does not involve any danger.

Lao-Tse's philosophy influenced Confucius and other Chinese philosophers, as well as Zen Buddhists (a branch of Buddhism originated in China).

Confucianism

Do not do to man what you do not wish for yourself

Confucius (551 - 479 BC) is an ancient thinker and philosopher of China. His teachings had a profound impact on the lives of China and the countries of East Asia, becoming the basis of a philosophical system and religion known as Confucianism.

Confucianism, like Taoism, was a philosophical and moral doctrine, which later became the main imperial religion of China for many centuries. It answered not so much the question of how the world works, but the question of how to live in this world.

In Confucianism, Sky is the supreme divine power that determines the fate of all life on Earth, hence the name of the country - "Celestial", and the title of its ruler - "Son of Heaven", preserved until the twentieth century.

In the Confucian canon, there are 22 basic concepts. I cite only a few of them.

1. 仁 (rén) - philanthropy, humanity, dignified, humane person, the core of the fetus, the core.

2. 義 (yì) - debt / justice, due justice, sense of duty, meaning, substance, friendly relations.

3. 禮 (lǐ) - ceremony, worship, etiquette, propriety, culture as the basis of the Confucian ideology, an offering, a gift.

4. 道 (dào) - Tao, Tao-path, Path, truth, method, rule, custom, morality.

5. (16) 三綱 (sāngāng) - the Three Foundations (the absolute power of the sovereign over the subject, the father over the son, the husband over the wife). Dong Chung-shu, a follower of Confucius, introduced the concept of 三綱 五 常 (sāngāngwǔcháng) —Sanguanchuan, "Three foundations and five unshakable rules" (subordination of the subject to the sovereign, subordination of the son to the father and wife to husband, humanity, justice, politeness, rationality and loyalty).

6. (18) 小人 (xiǎorén) - Xiaozen, a low man, a vile people, a small man, the common people, a craven man. Later, it

was used as a derogatory synonym for the pronoun "I" when referring to seniors (authorities or parents).

I cite several quotations and aphorisms of more than 1000 attributed to Confucius [3].

• In a country that is ruled well, they are ashamed of poverty. In a country that is ruled badly, they are ashamed of wealth.

• Control the people with dignity, and people will be respectful.

• Treat the people kindly, and people will work with diligence.

• Raise the virtuous and teach the unlearned, and people will trust you.

• Try to be at least a little kinder, and you will see that you will not be able to do a bad deed.

• The unshakable middle is the highest virtue of all, but it has long been rare among people.

• Someone asked: "Is it rightly said that evil must be paid with good?" The teacher said: "And then what is to pay for good? For evil you have to pay with justice, and for good with good."

• A wise man does not do to others what he does not want him to do.

• People want wealth and fame for themselves; if both cannot be obtained honestly, they should be avoided. People fear poverty and obscurity; if both cannot be avoided without losing honor, they should be accepted.

• Be hard on yourself and soft to others. So, you protect yourself from human hostility.

• The noble helps people to see the good in themselves and does not teach people to see the bad in themselves. A low person does the opposite.

• The noble one lives in harmony with everyone, and the low person is looking for his own kind.

• In a country where there is order, be bold in both actions and speeches. In a country where there is no order, be bold in actions, but circumspect in speeches.

• The noble thinks about his due. A low person thinks about what is profitable.

Happiness is when you are understood, great happiness is when you are loved, real happiness is when you love.

• A journey of a thousand miles begins with one step.

• In three ways, can we come to wisdom: first, by thinking, this is the most noble way; secondly, by imitation, this is the easiest path, and, thirdly, by experience, this is the hardest path.

• People spend their health to make money, and then spend money to restore health. • Thinking nervously about the future, they forget about the present, so they live neither in the present nor for the sake of the future. They live as if they will never die, and when they die, they understand that they have never lived.

Buddhism

Buddhism [4] emerged in the sixth century BC in India, and has now spread into the countries of South, Southeast, Central Asia and the Far East and has about 500-800 million followers.

Tradition connects the emergence of Buddhism with the name of Prince Siddhartha Gautama. His father hid bad things from Gautama, protected him from the knowledge of life outside the palace, with its suffering, illness and death. Gautama lived in luxury, married his girlfriend, who bore him a son.

The impetus for the spiritual revolution for the prince, as legend has it, was four meetings. At first, he saw a decrepit old man, then a leper and a funeral procession. So, Gautama learned old age, illness and death — the destiny of all people — and concluded that life is suffering. Then he saw a peaceful, poor wanderer, who needed nothing from life. All this shocked the prince, made him think about the fate of people. He secretly left the palace and family, in 29 years he became a hermit and tried to find the meaning of life. As a result of deep reflection at the age of 35, he became a Buddha — enlightened, awakened. For 45 years, the Buddha preached his doctrine, which can be briefly reduced to the doctrine of the four noble truths:

1. All human life - suffering

2. The cause of suffering is our desire

3. To get rid of suffering, you need to get rid of desire.

4. To get rid of desire, you need to go on the octal path of salvation, having mastered that, person can achieve mental and moral self-purification, peace and happiness.

Eightfold Path of Salvation:

1. The right way is to think about life, to see the world through the eyes of the Buddha — with wisdom and compassion.

2. Right thoughts. We are what we think. Clear and kind thoughts build good, strong characters.

3. Correct speech. For kind and helpful words, we are respected and trusted.

4. Proper behavior. Regardless of what we say, others judge us not by words, but by behavior. Before criticizing others, we must first see what we do ourselves.

5. The correct lifestyle. Do not do what hurts others. Buddha said, "Do not seek happiness by making others miserable."

6. Proper effort. To do everything possible, having good will towards others, not to waste efforts on what is to the detriment of oneself and others.

7. Proper Attention. It means to be aware of our thoughts, words and deeds.

8. Proper concentration. At each moment you need to focus

only on one thought or object.

Finally, we have five percepts (commandments):

1. Do not kill - Respect life
2. Do not steal - Respect the property of others
3. Do not do sexual harassment - Respect our pure nature
4. Don't Lie - Respect Honesty
5. Do not take intoxicants (alcohol, drugs, etc.) - Respect a clear mind

We can combine five Buddhist percepts into one:

"Respect yourself and your neighbor."

In Buddhism, there are no commandments about God, because there is no God in Buddhism, because Buddha is not God. Buddhists believe that there was no Creator, that is, the world has no end, no beginning.

Buddha says that people who live according to his teachings will enter into nirvana, a state without suffering, and in later works, nirvana was declared a state of permanent happiness.

Unlike monotheistic religions (Judaism, Christianity, Zoroastrianism, Islam), the following beliefs do not exist in Buddhism:

• the almighty creator god or personality god,
• the creation of the world - the world is considered "not created and not manageable"
• the eternal soul,
• atonement for sins,

• unconditional belief in supernatural forces
• absolute devotion to a religious organization similar to a church (the Buddhist sangha is a community, not an organization)
• heresies, for the reason that in Buddhism there is also no single canon of texts common to all schools (the common tripitak or a collection of all Buddhist texts in the last Mahayana Chinese edition is a 220-volume edition)
• a single universe, the number of worlds is considered infinite,
• common and indisputable dogmas for all schools,
• Providence, for which Buddhism is sometimes described as the "religion of salvation itself,"
• an indispensable refusal of a follower from other religions. A follower of Buddhism can be at the same time a follower of Shintoism, Taoism, and any other religion, without breaking the foundations of Buddhist teaching, which is one of the manifestations of Buddhist tolerance.

Eastern teaching about life

Taoism, Confucianism and Buddhism are the three major religions of East Asia. They preached the moral improvement of man and urged not to change the world, but to accept the world as it is. They preached obedience.

Aristotle described the Oriental form of monarchy as

Despotism [5], which exercised the power of a master over his servant who voluntarily or passively accept the despot power. Despotism, for Aristotle, was the most suitable form of government for nations having a natural tendency towards subordination. Therefore, such power is legitimate and hereditary, and the system is stable and durable. A despot governs not by laws, but by his or her own will and caprice.

The Russian philosopher Chaadaev wrote: "In the East, submissive minds, kneeling before historical authority, were exhausted in uncomplaining service to their sacred principle and eventually fell asleep, locked in their fixed synthesis."

6. ZOROASTRIANISM

Good thoughts, good speeches, good deeds
Man, in this universe was given the freedom to choose
between good and evil, truth and falsehood
Truth is the highest good
Those who choose the truth will become immortal. Lie will
be gone

Zarathustra [1], in Greek - Zoroaster, was one of the greatest thinkers of mankind, who created the religion of Zoroastrianism [2]. The Zoroastrian scripture is Avesta [3]. Atar (fire) is a primary symbol of Zoroastrianism.

Zarathustra was born in Iran (Persia). It is believed that he lived most likely in the sixth century BCE [1], although other sources, based on the linguistic features of the survived Zarathustra's texts, consider the time of his life to be around 1200 BCE [2].

During the reign of the Achaemenid dynasty (6th – 4th centuries BCE) Zoroastrianism occupied a dominant position in ancient Persia and finally took shape as a state religion under the Sassanids. The power and might of Persia have provided Zoroastrianism with enormous prestige and more than a thousand years of advancement. Arab expansion (VII-X century), marked the decline of Zoroastrianism. Muslims were extremely negative about Zoroastrianism. They forced the believers to convert to Islam. Many followers of Zoroastrianism gradually migrated to India, where they established their communities. The descendants of these migrants are currently living in India and Pakistan.

According to Zarathustra, the world was created by the God of Light, Ahura-Mazda (Wise Lord).

The God of Light is opposed by Angra-Mainyu - the principle of evil. If everything from the Ahura Mazda was noble and useful: the cultivated land, domestic animals, water, health, or daylight, then from the most important evil spirit - Angra Mainyu everything was dark and unclean: sins, deception, sorcery, death, illness, old age, decay, or rotting.

Zarathustra taught that man in this universe was given the freedom to choose between good and evil, truth and falsehood. So, the personal choice of people can predetermine the outcome of the world battle between good and evil, that is the fate of the world. Thus, the person became responsible for the world order. The struggle between good and evil is the content of world history. Each person must make his own choice and fight to hasten the victory of good over evil. Righteous acts strengthen Goodness and Truth. On the contrary, the bad actions of man intensify evil. In all the teachings of Zarathustra, Good and Truth are opposed to evil and lies. "As long as I have the strength and capabilities, I will teach people to strive for truth-asha".

Zoroastrians preached the cult of purity. Daily ablution was obligatory, but the main ceremony was the purification of the soul. One of the most effective ways to purify the soul and atone for sins is considered to be gratuitous and voluntary participation in socially useful works, such as laying canals, building bridges, plowing and loosening the land, and making tools. Charity and help to the poor were also important for cleansing.

The East Asian religions cited above preached the moral improvement of man and urged not to change the world, but to accept the world as it is, i.e. preached obedience. Contrary to their teaching, Zarathustra preached active participation of believers in everyday life of their community through social work, charity and help to poor. That attitude Jesus Christ named "love your neighbor". It is much more than the passive attitude *Do not do to man what you do not wish for yourself"*, proclaimed by Confucius in China and Socrates in Greece

Zarathustra introduced the concept of heaven and hell. After death, the Angels will lead all men and women through a narrow bridge. People who have chosen evil in life will fall into the abyss with burning fire, and the followers of Zarathustra will pass over the bridge to paradise.

At the end of the time there would be the Last Judgment. The scriptures offer a hope to everyone since the stay in heaven or hell is deemed temporary because the souls will once again be subjected to judgment by God. Before the Last Judgment all the dead will be resurrected. And then they will separate the sinners from the righteous. Sinners will be cast into hell, and the righteous will ascend to heaven. All sinners will be burned, and the righteous will live forever.

Zarathustra asked Ahura Mazda: "Where does the body come from, which was carried away by the wind and carried away by the water? How will the resurrection of the dead occur? "Ahura Mazda replied:" If I created the sky without columns on an invisible ("spiritual") basis ... if I created the Earth, which carries the entire material world ... if I sent the sun, the moon, and the stars into the sky... if I had created a son in the womb and separately created skin, nails, blood, eyes, ears and other parts of the body... Know that if I created something that was not, then why is it impossible for me to recreate what was?"[3]

Zarathustra's teaching was absolutely revolutionary for its time. In all early religions there were gods - patrons of some group of people. In Sumer and ancient Egypt, various gods were responsible for individual cities. Then in Egypt during the reign of Pharaoh Akhenaten only one god was recognized for the entire Egyptian people - the creator god Amon Ra. The Jews also had their own God, Yahweh. In all these teachings, God predetermined the fate of people, therefore rituals and sacrifices were important in order to appease God.

Zarathustra introduced monotheism, one God for the whole Earth. The doctrine equalized all nations and classes in the face of the Cosmos. It was the first universal religion. The origin and state did not matter, all had the same free will and moral choice, and the way to God did not lie through rites and sacrifices, but through "good thoughts, good speeches, good deeds".

The Eastern religions were telling "Do not do evil" - good, but passive attitude. Zarathustra said: "Choose Good and Truth and do Good." That is active attitude.
The ideas of Zoroastrianism formed the basis of Christianity and, through it, became the basis of modern Western civilization.

The changes that took place in the life of nations and states in the middle of first millennium BCE needed a revision of old polytheistic beliefs.

The Achaemenid Empire is an ancient state that existed in the 6th — 4th centuries BCE on the territory of Asia [4] was created by King Cyrus II the Great (593–529 BCE) and was the largest empire of the Ancient World. By the end of the VI century BC the boundaries of the Achaemenid Empire extended in the east from the Indus River to the Aegean Sea in the west, from the first Nile threshold in the south to the Transcaucasia in the north. Almost the entire population of South-West Asia has long needed a strong state capable of ensuring the security of trade routes and relative stability for merchants interested in expanding their trade and opening a market between the West and the East.

By joining the conquered lands to their state, the Persians did not destroy the conquered cities, but on the contrary, respected other people's traditions, faith and culture. By joining the lands of Palestine and Phoenicia to his possessions, King Cyrus restored Jerusalem and many Phoenician cities, allowed the Jews to return from their Babylonian captivity to their homeland and re-erect the Temple destroyed by the Babylonians.

In 515 BC Darius I built a road that went through the whole empire. The road with a length of two and a half thousand kilometers was called the "Royal Route."[5] It began in Sardis (about 90 km east of the modern city of Izmir in Turkey) and went east to the Assyrian capital Nineveh (the current Mosul in Iraq). Then, as it is believed, it was divided into two parts: one led to the east, through Ecbatana to the Silk Road, the other - to the south and southeast, to Susa and Persepolis. This road facilitated the exchange of not only goods, but also ideas.

A large number of peoples lived on this territory, with their tribal gods and beliefs. There was a need for a religion that unites the population of the empire. Such a religion was Zoroastrianism. It spread out quickly. Tsar Cyrus II the Great, who created the Persian Empire, and the subsequent Persian kings, preached Zoroastrianism, since Zoroastrianism was really a universal religion.

Zoroastrianism was different from all the religions that existed at that time. In those religions, little depended on man. Gods in ethnic religions predetermined the fate of man. Therefore, prayers and sacrifices to the gods were very important. Eastern religions, on the other hand, preached obedience and the preservation of existing conditions. Thus, man had to fulfill the will of the gods or the will of the higher, ruling class.

Zarathustra taught that man has the freedom of choice. He can choose between good and evil, between truth and falsehood. The teaching of Zarathustra gave man self-dependence.

From what choice a person made, his fate depended, as well as the fate of the whole world, since the choice of a person could increase either the general good and truth, or the general evil and lie.

The ideas of Zoroastrianism formed the basis of Christianity and because of that they became the basis of modern Western civilization.

Peter Chaadaev wrote: "... in the West, they (people) walked proudly and freely, bowing only before the authority of mind and heaven, stopping only before the unknown, constantly gazing into the unlimited future."

Part II

CHRISTIANITY

7. THE CREED OF JESUS CHRIST

The Holy Book of Christianity, The Bible, consists of the Old Testament, the holy book of the Jews, and the New Testament, the teachings of Jesus Christ. The New Testament consists of 27 books: the 4 Gospels (from Matthew, Mark, Luke and John), the Acts of the Apostles, the Epistles (21 letters, 14 of which belong to the Apostle Paul) and the Revelation of John the Theologian. The Gospel of John was written later than the first three, so-called synoptic Gospels, and differs from them.

Gospel in Greek means the good news.

The gospels describe the life of Jesus Christ, his divine nature, birth, miracles, his teachings, death, resurrection, and ascension.

What do we know about Jesus Christ? The birth of Jesus Christ from the Immaculate Virgin Mary is described in two Gospels: Matthew (1:18 - 2:23) and Luke (1:26 - 2:40).

Both Gospels say that the angel informed Mary of the immaculate conception and that she would give birth to the Son of God. Luke, in his gospel, says that when she heard this Annunciation from an angel, Mary went to Elizabeth, who at that moment was pregnant already in the sixth month. Mary stayed with Elizabeth for 3 months. Elizabeth gave birth to a son, who was named John who would later be called John the Baptist.

None of the gospels, with exception of Luke's, say anything about the childhood, adolescence, and youth of Jesus Christ. The only story about young Jesus is from Luke 2:41-52: When Jesus was twelve years old, his family went to Jerusalem for the Festival of the Passover. [43] *After the festival was over, while his parents were returning home, the boy Jesus stayed behind in Jerusalem, but they were unaware of it.* [45] *When they did not find him, they went back to Jerusalem to look for him.* [46] *After three days they found him in the temple courts, sitting among the teachers, listening to them and asking them questions.* [47] *Everyone who heard him was amazed at his understanding and his answers.*

In all four gospels Jesus begins his sermon as a mature man, about 32-33 years old. Therefore, it can be assumed that he and John the Baptist had previously traveled or, perhaps, worked or traded in Asia Minor and Europe. This can be argued on the grounds that the teaching of Jesus

Christ is based on the ideas of Zoroastrianism.

Trade in goods and the exchange of ideas went from India through the Persian Empire to Greece, Rome and further to the West. Philosophy, science, art and architecture were developing. New ideas, such as Zoroastrianism in the Persian Empire and democracy in Greece and Rome were seething.

There were integration processes arising from the exchange of products, worldviews, ideas and cultures. There was a need for a single faith for all peoples inhabiting the territory. Gradually, the ethnic gods were replaced by one God for all. It appears that during his journey, Jesus had the opportunity to get to know these ideas.

The Gospels of Mark and John begin with a story, as John the Baptist baptized the people of Judea and Jerusalem, declaring that not he himself, but Jesus, is the Messiah — the Christ, the messenger of God.

John baptized people by immersion in the Jordan River. Water was a symbol of purity in Zoroastrianism, and daily washing was the responsibility of the Zoroaster believer.

After the baptism by John, Jesus left for 40 days in the wilderness. He had to choose a road. He could choose "the spacious road of the slave passions," to which the devil tempted him. But he chose the road leading to "humiliated and offended," the road of the Messiah. Christ understood the heavy burden he had taken upon himself; he knew that he may undergo much of trials and even death. Returning from the desert, Jesus began to gather the disciples and preach.

There is the following scene in Matthew's Gospel (13: 54-56):

54 When he came to his hometown, he began to teach people in his synagogue, and they were amazed. "Where did this man get this wisdom and these wonderful powers?" They asked. "Is he not the son of a carpenter? Is it not the name of his mother, Mary, and not his brothers James, Joseph, Simon and Jude? 56 Are not all his sisters with him? Where, then, did this man get it all?

This scene can speak of the long absence of Jesus from his city. Although those present in the synagogue recognized him, but they wonder where he acquired all this wisdom, where he received all his strength. This did not happen in their city, before their eyes.

In addition, Jesus Christ sent the disciples to preach in Asia Minor, Greece and Rome. They became Apostles - missionaries of Jesus Christ (αποστολ - mission). The apostles had great success on the territory of the Roman Empire, because the ideas preached by Jesus must have been in the air at that time and were happily accepted by the people.

Sermons of Jesus Christ

1. One God for all people

The religion of Moses divided the whole world into Jews and non-Jews - Gentiles. The God of Jesus Christ is the God of all people — Jews and Gentiles. The God of Jesus Christ is a loving, kind god, to whom you can turn for help as to a father. He does not need sacrifices. It was the idea of Zoroastrianism - the only God for all people on Earth.

I give a few examples:

Jesus asks for water from a Samaritan woman, although he should not speak to her, and she explains to him that the Jews do not communicate with the Samaritans (John 4: 9).

Peter: *And he said to them: you know that Judea has been forbidden to communicate or get close to a foreigner; but the Lord revealed to me that I should not call anyone as profane or unclean.* (Acts 10:28)

And he said (Christ) to them (the disciples): Go all over the world and preach the gospel to all created things. (Mark 16:15)

Peter opened his mouth and said I truly know that God is impartial, but in every nation everyone who fears him and does what is right is acceptable to him. (Acts 10: 34-35)

When Peter continued this speech, the Holy Spirit fell on

all who listened to the word. And the believers of the circumcision, who came with Peter, were amazed that the gift of the Holy Spirit was poured out on the Gentiles. (Acts 10: 44-45)

Paul says: *The Lord commanded us to be a light for the Gentiles so that we would be saved to the ends of the earth. The Gentiles, hearing this, rejoiced and glorified the word of the Lord, and believed all who were granted unto eternal life.* (Acts 13: 47-48)

Is God the God of the Jews only, and not of the Gentiles also? Of course, Gentiles, too, because there is one God (Romans" 3:29)

Circumcision is nothing and uncircumcision is nothing. Keeping God's commands is what counts. (1 Corinthians 7:19)

2. Creation of the world

In the Gospel of John is given the creation of the world, different from that described in the Old Testament.

In the beginning was the Word, and the Word was with God, and the Word was God. It was in the beginning with God. All through Him began to be, and without Him nothing began to be, that began to be. (John 1.1-1.3).

This creation of the world is abstract and deep. In the beginning was the Word (maybe Thought, Idea? - GP), i.e.

something not material, that it is difficult to imagine.

John says that Jesus Christ is the light that God sent to earth. This is similar to the teaching of Zarathustra. "Ahura Mazda is a God omniscient and kind, forever dwelling in the light."

3.   Not keeping the Sabbath.

Jesus, who healed the sick, told him to take his bed and walk. But it was a Sabbath day and it was not permitted to wear a bed. The Jews were outraged and wanted to kill Jesus for not keeping the Sabbath. (John 5.6- 5.16)

For Jews, the Sabbath was dedicated to the God Yahweh. But Christ, like Zarathustra, preached the idea that one can receive eternal life for worthy behavior, and not through rites and rituals. Gospel of Mark 12:33 says: *To love him (God) with all your heart, with all your understanding and with all your strength, and to love your neighbor as yourself is more important than all burnt offerings and sacrifices."*

4.   Cancellation of the ritual of cooking and food consumption

Jewish law gives instructions on what products may or may not be eaten, and how these products should be prepared. There were many dietary restrictions in Judaism.

For example, it was allowed to eat meat of only artiodactyl, herbivores. Pork was not allowed to eat, since the pig is omnivorous. The meat of cloven-hoofed ruminants (cow) was allowed. Restrictions have also been imposed on fish, poultry, insects, drinks and other types of products. These limitations were ritual rather than experiential. In Islam, as in Judaism, it is forbidden to eat pork, but it is allowed to eat beef. Some other religions have other restrictions, for example, in Hinduism and Buddhism it is forbidden to eat beef, which is allowed in Judaism, and it is allowed to eat pork, which is forbidden in Judaism and Islam.

All dietary restrictions given by Moses were abolished in Christianity.

He (Peter) became hungry and wanted something to eat, and while the meal was being prepared, he fell into a trance. [11] He saw heaven opened and something like a large sheet being let down to earth by its four corners.[12] It contained all kinds of four-footed animals, as well as reptiles and birds. [13] Then a voice told him, "Get up, Peter. Kill and eat." [14] "Surely not, Lord!" Peter replied. "I have never eaten anything impure or unclean." [15] The voice spoke to him a second time, "Do not call anything impure that God has made clean. (Acts 10: 10-15)

5. Love of neighbor

The basis of Moses teachings was the worship of the God Yahweh through rituals, prohibitions and offerings, and observance of laws: the 10 commandments, as well as many other laws relating to all aspects of life.

Jesus Christ preached two commandments:

1. *Love the Lord your God with all your heart, and with all your soul, and with all your mind.* This commandment corresponds to the commandments of 1-3 Moses.

2. *Love your neighbor as yourself* (includes the commandments 5-10 of Moses and many other good commandments).

Moses has the similar law: *Do not revenge, and do not bear malice **on the sons of your people** (singled out by GP), but love your neighbor as yourself* (Leviticus 19:18). In Judaism, this law applies only to the people of Israel, while the commandment of Jesus applies to all.

So, in everything you want people to do with you, so do you with them, for this is the law and the prophets. (Matthew 7: 5)

6. Nonresistance to evil by violence

The law of Moses "an eye for an eye and a tooth for a tooth," read:

"23 ... if it hurts, give soul for soul

24 eyes for eyes, tooth for tooth, hand for hand, foot for leg

25 burning for burning, wound for wound, bruise for bruise.

(Exodus 21: 23-27) "

This law was rejected by Jesus Christ. Jesus preached Love, humility, mercy, compassion, grace, repentance, forgiveness, justice and peace, all that is now called Western values.

The Sermon on the Mount (Matthew's Gospel, Chapter 5)

1. Having seen the people, he went up to the mountain; and when he sat down, his disciples came to him.
2. And He, having opened His mouth, taught them, saying:
3. Blessed are the poor in spirit, for theirs is the kingdom of heaven.
4. Blessed are those who mourn, for they will be comforted.
5. Blessed are the meek, for they shall inherit the earth.
6. Blessed are they who hunger and thirst for righteousness, for they shall be filled.
7. Blessed are the merciful, for they will be shown mercy.
8. Blessed are the pure in heart, for they shall see God.
9. Blessed are the peacemakers, for they will be called the

sons of God.

10. Blessed are those who are cast out for righteousness, for theirs is the kingdom of heaven.

11. Blessed are you when others revile you and persecute you and utter all kinds of evil against you falsely on my account.

12. Rejoice and be glad, for your reward is great in heaven, for so they persecuted the prophets who were before you.

16. Let your light so shine before men, that they may see your good works and glorify your Father who is in heaven.

17. Do not think that I came to break the law or the prophets, I did not come to break, but to fulfill.

38. You have heard that it was said: an eye for an eye and a tooth for a tooth.

39. But I say unto you Do not resist the one who is evil. But whoever slaps you on your right cheek, turn the other to him.

40. And whoever wants to sue you and take your shirt from you, give him your outer clothing too;

41. and who will force you to go one mile, go with him two.

42. Give to him who asks from you, and do not turn away from those who want to borrow from you.

43. You have heard that it is said: love your neighbor and hate your enemy.

44. And I say to you: love your enemies, bless those who curse you, do good to those who hate you and pray for those who offend you and persecute you

45. That you may be sons of your Father in heaven, for he commands his sun to rise above the evil and good and sends rain on the just and the unjust.

46. For if you love those who love you, what is your reward? Do not tax collectors do the same

47. And if you greet only your brothers, what are you doing special?

48. Be therefore perfect, as your Heavenly Father is perfect.

Like Zarathustra, Jesus Christ pays great attention to the concept of Truth: *Actually, I was born and came into the world to testify to the truth. All who love the truth recognize that what I say is true.* says Jesus to Pilate. (John 18:37)

Jesus, like Zarathustra, says that there will be a final judgment. Before the judgment, all the dead will be resurrected. And then they will separate the sinners from the righteous. Sinners will be cast into hell, and the righteous will ascend to heaven. All sinners will be burned, and the righteous will live forever.

I cite a few quotes:

So, it will be at the end of the age, the angels will come forth and separate the evil from among the righteous. And they shall be cast into the furnace of fire. (Matthew 13: 49-50)

And these shall go into everlasting torment, but the righteous shall live eternal. (Matthew 25:46)

For all of us must come before the judgment of Christ, that each may receive according to what he did while living in a body, good or bad. (2 Corinthians 5:10)

In the Bible at different times, the prophets predicted the coming of the Messiah. Jesus claims that he is the Messiah: *Do not think that I have come to break the law or the prophets, I have not come to break, but to fulfill,* - Jesus says in the Sermon on the Mount. But the Jews did not recognize in Jesus the Messiah - Christ. *No prophet is accepted in his hometown.* (Mark 3:21)

8. THE SPREAD OF CHRISTIANITY

Christianity first gradually spread throughout the predominantly Greek-speaking eastern part of the Roman Empire. The apostles traveled throughout the empire, creating communities in large cities and regions. The first Christian communities appear in Jerusalem, and then in Antioch, Ethiopia and other areas. Communities appeared in the political centers of Greece and in Rome, as well as in Byzantium. Historically, the word "church" did not mean a building (for which the Greeks used the word "basilica") but meant a community or a congregation.

By tradition, it is believed that the Greek communities were established by the Apostle Paul. Antioch, and Asia Minor churches, are the institution of the Apostle Peter. The Church of Rome was founded by Peter and Paul. The Coptic (or Egyptian communities) were founded by the Apostle Mark (including in Ethiopia and Abyssinia).

Assyrian, Byzantine and Georgian churches were founded by Apostle Andrew.

The Armenian Church was founded by the Apostles Thaddeus and Bartholomew.

In their sermons the Apostles dissociated themselves from the teachings of Moses. In his letters, the Apostle Paul preaches the ideas of Christianity and criticizes the laws of Moses. For example, in a letter to Galatians, Paul says:

1: 3 *Grace to you and peace from God, our Father, and the Lord Jesus Christ. All people are equal before God.*

3:28 There is neither Jew nor Gentile; no slave, no free; there is neither male nor female: for you are all one in Christ Jesus.

Paul believes that complying with church laws and rituals makes people slaves of their gods.

4: 8 In the past, when you did not know God, you were slaves to gods, who are not gods.

4: 9 But now you know the true God (or rather, you have become known to God)! Why, then, do you return to these pathetic, useless laws that you are trying to serve again?

5: 1 Christ has set us free so that we may live free.

5: 2 Listen! I, Paul, tell you: if you return to the fold of the law through circumcision, then you will have no benefit from Christ! So, remain firm and do not reinstate the burden of slavery again.

5: 3 I say again to all those who allow themselves to be

circumcised that they are obliged to abide by the whole law.

5: 4 Those of you who try to declare yourself to be righteous through observance of the law have nothing to do with Christ. Now you are beyond the grace of God.

5: 6 For before Jesus Christ neither circumcision nor uncircumcision has power, but only faith manifested in deeds committed in love.

5:13 But you, brothers, were called by God to live free. However, let not freedom be for you a reason to satisfy your sinful nature! Instead, serve each other with love.

5:14 For the whole law is reduced to one statement, which says: "Love your neighbor as yourself."

5: 22-23 But the spirit produces love, joy, peace, patience, kindness, trust, meekness, and temperance. There is no law against such things.

6:10 And so, since we have the opportunity, we will do good to all people, and especially to our brothers in faith.

6:15 For neither circumcision nor uncircumcision means anything. It is only important that you become the new creation of God.

9. EARLY CHRISTIANITY

Initially, Christianity was the religion of the oppressed, mostly slaves and soldiers. They were impressed by equality, brotherhood and love of neighbor. But gradually the civilian base expanded and in the 4th century one of the most remarkable historical events was the transition in 312 AD of Roman emperor Constantine the Great (reign 306–337 AD) to Christianity. Christianity began to move into the dominant religion of the Roman Empire.

Emperor Theodosius I made Christianity the state religion of the Roman Empire in 380 A D.

Thus, over the course of several hundred years, a small, often brutally persecuted cult grew to become the dominant religion in the West.

At first, the whole church was called Catholic, which in Greek means single, universal, all-encompassing. The church was ruled by five bishops (Rome, Constantinople,

Jerusalem, Alexandria, Antioch).

After the Theodosius I death in 395, the empire was finally divided into the western part with the capital in Rome and the eastern part with the capital in Constantinople, later called Byzantium. Although unofficially so far, the church was also divided into a Western one with a Roman bishop and an Eastern one with 4 bishops (Constantinople, Jerusalem, Alexandria, Antioch).

In 476 the Western Roman Empire fell from the constant invasions of barbarians. The period of economic and cultural deterioration began, which lasted for more than 5 centuries. But gradually in Europe, new states were formed, agriculture and crafts developed, trade in the Mediterranean began to grow, education raised, and universities appeared. A university was opened in Bologna, Italy, in 1088 and in Oxford, England, in 1096. In the 12th century, a university was opened in Paris. In the 13th century, universities were organized in Vicenza (Italy), in Cambridge, and another 13 universities throughout Europe. The Renaissance began. In the 14th century, another 16 universities appeared, including universities in central and eastern Europe: Prague (1348), Krakow (1364), Pec in Hungary (1367), Zadar in Croatia (1396). In the 15th century, another 28 universities were opened. The revival in Europe was in full swing.

Disagreements between the western and eastern

churches on dogmatic and liturgical issues have always been. These differences intensified, and in 1054 the church finally broke up into a Catholic, led by the Pope and the Orthodox, led by the Patriarch.

10. CHRISTIANITY AFTER THE SPLIT

Orthodox Church

The dogmas of the Orthodox Church were established during the 7 Ecumenical Councils, which were held from the 4th to the 8th century AD [1].

These Ecumenical Councils with their doctrines are key to the history of the Orthodox Church. They represent a permanent standard for the Orthodox understanding of the Trinity, the person or hypostasis of Christ, the Incarnation, Heaven, Hell, etc.

An Orthodox rite established at the Ecumenical Councils was the so-called Byzantine rite. The ceremony consists of divine liturgy, the administration of sacred secrets (sacraments), numerous prayers and blessings, as well as the ritual of expelling an evil spirit from a person or place. The rite also established the specifics of architecture, icons, liturgical music and clothing. Traditionally, the chief clergy and monks were not supposed to shave and cut their hair or beards.

The iconostasis separates the altar from the nave of the church. Ritually, believers stand throughout the entire service. Believers are very active during their service, they make frequent bows, cross themselves, stay on their knees and prostrate.

A church calendar was established. Many church traditions, including service schedules, festivals, and fasts, are structured according to the calendar, and prayers to saints were instituted.

Religious authority for Orthodoxy was not the Bible, but the Scripture as interpreted by the seven Ecumenical Councils, rituals and rites established at these Councils [1–4]. Thus, the Orthodox Church departed from the teachings of Jesus Christ, immersed in the formal performance of rituals.

After the split with the Catholic Church, Constantinople patriarchate started to govern all orthodox Church.

There were only two languages used: Greek in the Orthodox and Latin in Catholic Church.

In 863 Cyril and Methodius, Constantinople missionaries, started their work among the Slavs, using Slavonic language in the liturgy [5]. They translated the Bible into the language later known as Old Church Slavonic (or Old Bulgarian) and invented the Glagolitic alphabet, a Slavic alphabet based on Greek characters that in its final Cyrillic form is still in use as the alphabet for modern Russian, Belarusian, Ukrainian, Bulgarian, Macedonian, and Serbian. All of these nations belong to Orthodox Church today.

Catholic Church

Separation from the Christian doctrine occurred in the Catholic Church, as well. The Catholic Church organized several Crusades (from 1096 to 1487), including a children's Crusade (1212), when almost all the children died. This violated the commandment "do not kill".

Church robbed and exploited believers. Expensive church temples were built. Higher clergy lived in luxury, breaking the Christian commandment not to accumulate material wealth. In the divine service many rites were used, the priests wore rich robes, there were many statues in the churches. In the Vatican the church of St. Peter was built, the largest in the world. The popes wanted to show their earthly power. The church actively participated in state affairs, violating the covenant of Christ: *Render to Caesar the things that are Caesar's; and to God the things that are God's.* (Romans 13:1) In the Vatican, indulgences were sold — papers in which the names of loved ones, dead or living, could be written. It was alleged that indulgence opens the way to paradise, bypassing purgatory. So, it was advertised papal sellers. Indulgences were first issued for participants in the Crusades, and later they were sold to everyone.

At this time, both the Orthodox and the Catholic Churches could be called Christian only with a great stretch - they were deeply corrupt. Both practically turned into religions, gone far from the teachings of Jesus Christ. The covenants of Christ were not kept.

11. REFORMATION AND PROTESTANTISM

Beginning of the reformation

It became clear to the enlightened people of Europe that it was necessary to revive the Christian faith. This was not easy to do because the church demanded absolute obedience and declared all dissidents to be heretics and executed. The movement for the return of the Catholic Church to its origins began in Italy [6].

Francis of Assisi (1181-1226)

When the Crusades were in full swing Francis of Assisi began to preach obedience, humility, simplicity, rejection of any privileges, and equality between people, spiritual renewal. Young Francis lived among patients with leprosy. The confession of the gospel and the apostolic calling gathered many followers around him. Later, the Franciscan Monastic Order was organized and indicated by its example the path to renewing the Church and returning to spiritual life. In Europe, a movement began to revive the church by returning to the gospel. The Dominican Order, the Order of St. Augustine, and others were created. They taught the Gospel, preached chastity, a proportional distribution of labor, fraternal love and care for the sick.

John Wycliffe (1331-1384)

One of the first predecessors of the Reformation was the English philosopher, theologian, professor at Oxford University, John Wycliffe. Wycliff considered the Bible as the only reliable guide in the truth about God, and argued that Christians should rely on the Bible, and not on the teachings of the popes and the holy ministers. Wycliffe rejected the concept of purgatory, and did not approve of celibacy, pilgrimage, the sale of indulgences and prayers to the saints.

In the Catholic Church, all books, including the Bible and all church services, were in Latin. Wycliffe believed that the Bible should be translated into all languages and dialects, so that people could understand and judge their own faith. Wycliffe himself translated the New Testament into English. The Old Testament was translated under his supervision by his disciples and admirers.

After Wycliffe's death in 1384, his ideas quickly spread. The church declared him a heretic in 1415 and his writings were banned. It was decided to burn the philosopher and his works. This decision was carried out in 1428. The Wycliffe's remains were exhumed, burned, and the ashes were thrown into the river.

Jan Hus (1369 -1415)

Jan Hus is regarded as one of the earliest known religious thinkers and reformers. In 1396, Hus received a master's degree from Charles University in Prague and became a professor of theology.

The teachings of John Wycliffe had a strong influence on Hus. He, like John Wycliffe, preached that Christ, and not the pope, was the true head of the Church, that the church authorities should exercise spiritual power. He argued that neither the pope nor the bishop had the right to raise the sword in the name of the Church. He believed that a person can achieve forgiveness only by repentance. Hus also believed that everyone should have a Bible in their own language. He preached the need for reform in order to eradicate corruption and abuse in the Roman Church. His followers burned papal bulls because they considered Hus to be more correct.

Hus was arrested. Even his chapel was destroyed. During the trial, Hus sticks to only one argument, that he will repent if his mistakes are proved by quotations from the Gospel. Although there were several attempts, including torture, to force him to renounce his words and views, Hus did not do this and was sentenced to be burned. Already at the stake, Hus was asked for the last time if he would like to recant and save his life. Hus did not renege his views and was burned. After the execution of Hus, his followers (the Hussites) rebelled against the Catholic Church and won in five successive papal crusades (1420-1431). Pope Martin V issued a papal bull allowing the murder of all supporters of Hus and Wycliffe. 100 years after the death of Hus, only 10% of the Czech population remained in the Catholic faith.

Francysk Skaryna (1490 - 1552)

Francysk Skaryna is the founder of the Belarusian literary language, educator, contemporary of Martin Luther. He was born in Polotsk, Belarus, in the family of a merchant. He studied at the Jagiellonian University in Krakow and at the University of Padua, Italy. He translated the Bible into the Belarusian language. He opened a printing house in Prague, where he printed 22 books of the Bible with a total circulation of 2500 copies. When the persecution of reformers began in the Czechia, he moved to Vilnius. His printing house in Vilnius burned down during a big fire in 1525. He traveled to Moscow to sell his printed books and earn money to restore the burnt-out workshop. But in Moscow his books were burned, and he miraculously escaped. At the end of his life he worked in Prague.

Martin Luther (1483 - 1546)

Martin Luther was a German professor of theology, priest, translator of the Gospel into German, and a composer. Luther rejected many of the teachings and practices of the Catholic Church which contradicted the gospel. He was the initiator of the Protestant Reformation.

Martin Luther was born in Eisleben, Saxony, which was then part of the Holy Roman Empire. In 1501, at the age of 19, he entered the university in Erfurt and received a master's degree in 1505. In accordance with the wishes of his father, Luther entered the law school at the same university, but dropped out almost immediately, because he was interested in theology and philosophy. In 1507, Luther was anointed as a priest, and in 1508 he was invited to the University of Wittenberg. He received a bachelor's degree in biblical studies, and in 1512 received a doctorate in theology and became a professor of theology at the theological faculty of the University of Wittenberg, where he worked until the end of his life.

Luther made a translation of the Bible into German, which played a huge role in the formation of the German literary language.

In 1517, Pope Leo X issued a bulla about the sale of indulgences and absolution in order to "assist in the construction of Saint Peter's Basilica and the salvation of the souls of Christendom. " Luther rejects the role of the church in salvation and criticizes the dogmas of the Catholic Church, which he expresses in 95 theses [7]. The theses were printed and spread throughout Europe in 2-3 months. Luther criticizes the sale of indulgences and affirms the priority of the Gospel. A few examples from the Theses:

1. Our Lord and Master Jesus Christ, in saying, "Repent ye, etc.," intended that the whole life of his believers on earth should be a constant penance.

6. The Pope can forgive sins only in the sense, that he declares and confirms what may be forgiven of God; or that he doth it in those cases which he hath reserved to himself; be this contemned, the sin remains unremitted.

21. Therefore, those preachers of indulgences err who say that, by the Pope's indulgence, a man may be exempt from all punishments, and be saved.

24. Therefore the multitude is misled by the boastful promise of the paid penalty, whereby no manner of

distinction is made.

27. They preach vanity who say that the soul flies out of Purgatory as soon as the money thrown into the chest rattles. 28. What is sure, is, that as soon as the penny rattles in the chest, gain and avarice are on the way of increase; but the intercession of the church depends only on the will of God Himself.

36. Every Christian who feels sincere repentance and woe on account of his sins, has perfect remission of pain and guilt even without letters of indulgence.

43. Christians should be taught, he who gives to the poor, or lends to a needy man, does better than buying indulgence.

45. Christians should be taught, he who sees his neighbor in distress, and, nevertheless, buys indulgence, is not partaking in the Pope's pardons, but in the anger of God.

50. Christians should be taught, if the Pope knew the ways and doings of the preachers of indulgences, he would prefer that St. Peter's Minster should be burnt to ashes, rather than that it should be built up of the skin, flesh, and bones of his lambs.

55. The opinion of the Pope cannot be otherwise than this: If an indulgence - which is the lowest thing - be celebrated with one bell, one procession and ceremonies, then the Gospel - which is the highest thing - must be celebrated with a hundred bells, a hundred processions, and a hundred

ceremonies.

62. The right and true treasure of the Church is the most Holy Gospel of the glory and grace of God.

Rumors about theses spread sweepingly and in 1519 Luther was first summoned to the court and later to the Leipzig dispute. Luther arrived at the dispute despite the fate of Jan Hus. In the dispute he doubted the righteousness and infallibility of the Catholic papacy. Then Pope Leo X given Luther an anathema and in 1520 made a profanity bull.

Luther publicly burned the papal bull Domini excommunicating him in the courtyard of the University of Wittenberg. He appealed "To the Christian Nobility of the German Nation," announcing that the fight against papal domination is the work of the whole German nation.

Martin Luther said that besides the practice of baptism and communion, Christians must know the prayer "Our Father", the Symbol of Faith and the Ten Commandments.

The fundamental principles for the attainment of salvation according to the teachings of Luther: only faith, only grace, and only Holy Scripture. Luther declared insolvent the Catholic dogma that the church and the clergy are necessary mediators between God and man.

The only way to save the soul for a Christian is faith, bestowed upon him directly by God. "Man saves the soul not through the Church, but through faith," wrote Luther.

Priests are not mediators between God and man, they should only direct the flock and be an example of true Christians. Luther dismisses the divinity of the pope.

Luther formulated "Christian freedom" in this way: the freedom of the soul does not depend on external circumstances, but exclusively on the will of God. In contrast to the Catholic doctrine of opposing the worldly and the spiritual, Luther believed that God's grace was practiced in the worldly life and preached equality. God intends people to this or that kind of activity, investing in them various talents or abilities, and the duty of a person to work hard, fulfilling his vocation. In the eyes of God, there is no work noble or contemptible. "The works of the monks and priests, no matter how heavy and holy they are, are not one iota different in the eyes of God from the works of a peasant in the field or a woman working in the household," said Luther.

Martin Luther married Katharine von Bohr in 1525, they had 6 children. Their marriage was happy. Luther's wedding was the basis for the approval of the church marriage of all priests.

Luther defended basic Christian values such as love, patience, mercy, and freedom, and reminded citizens to trust in the Word of God.

The Peasant War in Germany (1524-1525)

In 1524-1525 peasant revolts began to flare up throughout the Holy Roman Empire [8]. Peasants burned churches, monasteries, palaces of bishops, libraries; destroyed icons and statues of saints. Under the leadership of radicals such as Thomas Muntzer in Thuringia and Michael Gaismair in Tyrol, riots escalated into war. The uprising of the German peasants was the largest and most widespread popular uprising in Europe preceding the 1789 French Revolution. The uprising began with the demand of the Reformation of the Catholic Church according to Luther, but it went beyond the framework of these requirements, including many economic and social problems of that time.

At this time, relations between the estates were built vertically. The peasants were vassals of the landowner, the landowner in turn was a vassal of the prince, and the prince was a vassal of the king. Therefore, not only peasants participated in the uprising, but also higher classes who fought for the expansion of their freedoms.

On March 6-7, 1525, a congress of representatives of the peasant detachments of Upper Swabia was held in Memmingen and the program "Twelve Articles" was adopted [9]. This document has survived 23 editions carried out in different German cities. It addressed religious and organizational issues, as well as the economic demands of the peasants.

The first article is devoted to the rights and duties of the parish priest. Each church community has "the right and the power of the whole community to choose a priest for themselves and to dislodge him when he is inappropriately behaving." The article also states that the priest must preach "a pure Gospel, without human addition," according to Martin Luther's reformatory thesis.

The second article is devoted to tithing. Although the compilers claim that tithing was fair in Old Testament times, and with the advent of the New Testament "lost its power", they are still ready to give "just grain tithe", but with the condition that it will be collected by church elders chosen by the entire community and that the collected funds will be paid sufficient maintenance to the priest and his relatives, and the remnants will be distributed to the poor members of the community, and the remaining money will be saved.

The third article is devoted to personal dependence: "It has so far been customary to regard us as 'own' people, which is pity like, considering that Christ, by spilling His precious blood, freed and redeemed all of us, - both the shepherd and the highest excluding anyone. Therefore, it corresponds to the scriptures so that we are and want to be free." Further, it is stipulated that the compilers do not reject the law and authority, but want to live by the law, and not by a free human fabrication.

In articles 4-12, economic requirements were put forward: repeal of laws according to which ordinary people were forbidden to freely catch game, poultry and fish and freely use forests, as well as to reduce excessive extortion and fines.

On the relationship between the master and the peasant, it was said: From now on, the peasant receives land from his master and owns it based on an agreement with the master. The lord has no right to demand any additional work from the peasant and should not force him to do anything so that the peasant can safely and without burdens use the land. It was necessary to establish a rent in justice "in such a way that the peasant would not do his work for nothing, for each worker is worthy of his pay."

Luther was sympathetic to the demands of the rebels, but categorically condemned the violence. He believed that it was unacceptable to resort to violence in order to achieve the necessary changes. Luther said that baptism does not make people free in the body and property, but in the soul; and the Gospel does not make property common, except when, of their own will, people make their property common, as the apostles and disciples did in Acts [4: 32-37].

Protestant denominations

Luther argued that everyone had the right to their own understanding and interpretation of the Gospel, so the charge of heresy became out of the question, which caused the formation of many Protestant denominations. They do not always agree with each other on all issues, but they recognize the main truths of the Christian faith. In the world there are several thousand Protestant denominations. The largest of them are Lutherans, Anglicans. Baptists, Methodists, Presbyterians, Evangelicals, Calvinists, etc., number tens and even hundreds of millions. There are small denominations with tens of thousands of believers. A list of the main Protestant denominations in the world is given on this site [10]. I will tell about two small Protestant denominations.

Quakers

Quakers (Brothers) believe that all people are equal in the eyes of God. [11] Since all people embody the divine spark, they deserve equal treatment. The Quakers believe that in the eyes of God there is no hierarchy based on birth, wealth, or political power. The Quakers were among the first to choose women as priests and advocate for the rights of women; they were leaders in the fight against slavery.

They were pioneers in the humane treatment of people with mental disorders, as well as prisoners. Quakers refuse to participate in the war, wore simple clothes, refuse to take oaths and swears, believe that they should not bow to anyone and take off their hat, regardless of title or rank, completely abstain from alcohol. In 2012, there were 377,000 Quakers around the world.

Amish

The Amish [12] movement began in Switzerland, and at the beginning of the 18th century, some of them moved to America and settled in Pennsylvania. Now they dwell in all the eastern and central states. The Amish now live just like their ancestors who came to America. They do not have electricity, that is, there are no televisions, telephones, refrigerators, etc. They work and ride horses, and do not use any chemistry. Amish do not pay taxes, because they themselves take care of their sick and old people, their roads and schools, and do not require any help from the state. Upon reaching the age of 18, each Amish has the right to "go into the world" for one year. If he returns (9 out of 10 do), he is baptized into Amish faith and remains in the community. Several feature films and documentaries were made about the life of the Amish. Now in America there are 249,000 Amish.

Significance of the Reformation

The Reformation was one of the most important events in the history of Western Europe. Christians were divided into Catholics and Protestants. Religious unity fell apart.

The Reformation was prepared by the ideas of the Renaissance. But, while the ideas of the Renaissance lived and developed in a narrow circle of educated people, the Reformation embraced the broad masses of the people and put into practice the ideas of justice, freedom and equality.

The ideas of Protestantism led to the beginning of individual thought and individual opinions regarding religion. Inevitably, this led to free thinking in other areas, such as politics, economics, and social structure. Many saw this change as an opportunity to gain greater control over their lives, which led to the mass popularity of free-thinking ideas. The Reformation sent history into the mainstream of freedom and thus marked the beginning of modern Western civilization.

For many centuries law codes of different countries were determined by moral precepts of religions, thus influencing their civil life. But the influences of the governing bodies on the religious life of people might also be strong. The religious life in United States and Russia will be discussed in order to demonstrate this affirmation.

12. RELIGION IN THE USA

Constitution of the United States of America

Starting from the 17th century, Protestants, often persecuted in their own countries, began to move to America. In 1789, America adopted a Constitution based on the Christian values of Protestants, as well as on the "Great Charter of Liberties" (Magna Carta), which was adopted in England in 1215 and said:

"No free man shall be seized or imprisoned, or stripped of his rights or possessions, or outlawed or exiled, or deprived of his standing in any other way, nor will we proceed with force against him, or send others to do so, except by the lawful judgement of his equals or by the law of the land. "

The Bill of rights of the USA Constitution (Amendments 1-10) was designed to guarantee and safeguard individual freedom and protect citizens from excess government power.

According to the Amendment I, Congress shall make no law respecting an establishment of religion or prohibiting the free exercise thereof; or abridging the freedom of speech, or of the press; or the right of the people peaceably to assemble, and to petition the government for a redress of grievances.

The constitution contains the right of citizens to protect their free state. The second amendment to the Constitution states: "A well-organized police force is necessary for the security of a free state; the right of the people to keep and bear arms should not be violated." The federal government, as well as the states, do not have the legal power to disarm people from whom armed groups, militia, can be organized to protect a free state.

The Constitution prohibited the granting and use of aristocratic and noble titles, like the Earl, Prince, etc., and prohibited the use of respectful forms of addressing the aristocracy and nobility, like Your Highness, Your Excellency, etc. President should be addressed as Mr. President. An amendment adopted in 1810 stated that a US citizen who would take the aristocratic title from some foreign state would be deprived of US citizenship. The creators of the Constitution believed that noble titles should not take place in an equal and fair society.

"We hope and believe that the Constitution can contribute to the lasting well-being of this country, so dear to all of us, and ensure its freedom and happiness," wrote George Washington, the first president.

All 43 US presidents, except for catholic John F. Kennedy, were Protestants.

Presbyterians, Baptists, Methodists, and other confessions fought for equality and the abolition of slavery. Slavery in America was abolished in 1865.

The American Constitution is strictly enforced and implemented, as it is based on the moral values of the people.

Religion in the USA today

A detailed study of religious beliefs in the United States was conducted by Pew Research Center [9]. There are some survey data:

In God believe 83% of respondents.

Christians make up 70.6% of the population - of which Protestants 46%, Catholics 20.6%, Orthodox 0.5%

The significance of religion in a person's life:

Very important 53%

Fairly important 24%

Not too important 11%

Not important at all 11%

Participation in religious services:

at least once a week, 36%

once or twice a month 33%

rarely / never 30%

Thus, the church is one of the most important social organizations.

As an example, I describe churches in a university city, Columbia, MO.

The city has a University with 35 thousand students and 2 colleges, with 8 thousand students in each. The city has 110 thousand inhabitants, of which 55% have a higher education. There are more than 500 churches in the city and new ones are being built, since the city is growing.

The church is separated from the state. The church lives on money donated by the parishioners. And this is big money and people give them, because the church occupies an important place in their lives and the lives of their children. Churches are teaching how to live, that is, they teach Christian values. In addition, churches are actively involved in the life of the congregation.

In the city, except for the Protestant churches, which are the majority, there are 9 Catholic, one Greek Orthodox, one synagogue and one mosque.

Historical Orthodox and Catholic churches were built according to a strict plan: altar, prayer hall, and porch. Nothing directly related to the church service was allowed in the church building.

There are no restrictive rules for the construction of Protestant churches. Usually the church consists of an open altar, prayer hall and many other rooms and halls. Usually these are classes and rooms for children, rooms for clubs, a library, accounting room, a kitchen, a large dining room, where all the parishioners gather often.

In Protestant churches, worship is usually held as follows: the service takes place once a week, on Sunday, and lasts for one hour. Initially, the priest talks about what happened in the church and in the life of the congregation over the past week, as well as plans for the next week. Then they read "Our Father", the only prayer of the Protestant church. After that, the priest tells a sermon. During the service, the whole church sings a few songs. Everything is simple, no crosses, bows, no rituals.

During worship, children usually go to rooms for children and classes. Little kids play. The big ones study the Bible, which is taught at their level. All teachers are volunteers.

The main idea of education is to develop self-esteem in a person. The child is told that he is born to be happy, and that everyone around him should be happy too. The child must treat himself with respect, not lie, not steal, help the weak, etc., and then everyone will respect him. Approximately the same scheme of education is applied in school. The main task of education is to teach children to distinguish good from evil and live a dignified life.

At school it is strictly forbidden to show a student's marks to other students. Only parents know the ratings. This is done in order not to belittle a weak child, because he may lose respect for himself, consider himself unworthy of other children. The goal of the teacher is to help children find their strength, their talent. Some children draw well, others like mathematics, others build something, etc.

Schools teach children to understand and appreciate Christian values - love of neighbor, tolerance, respect for oneself and others, respect for one's own and others' freedom.

13. ORTHODOX CHURCH IN THE SECOND MILLENNIUM CE

Orthodox church is practiced in Greece, Romania and Slav language countries: Russia, Belarus, Ukraine, Bulgaria, Serbia, Croatia, Slovenia and Macedonia.

Orthodox church history of these countries varies from one country to another and depends much on their political development, because the Orthodox Church usually closely collaborated with the lay authorities. The time of the Bible translation in the languages of the Orthodox countries can confirm the above statement:

Bulgaria (Old Slavonic Language)   IX century
Serbia   1186
Belarus   1517-1525
Ukraine   XVI century (4 Gospels)
Romania   1661- 1668
Macedonia   1852

Before the Bible translations in the vernacular languages the liturgy was performed in the Old Church Slavonic unknown to the general public.

An important characteristic of the Orthodox church is the monastic life. The monasteries were also in the Catholic countries but not that numerous.

Russian writer F. M. Dostoevsky discussed the monastery life in his novel "The Brothers Karamazov".

The elder monk Zosima is described in the novel as its wise man, guru, and moral center.

Zosima says about monks:

"Meanwhile, in their solitude, they keep the image of Christ fair and undefiled, in the purity of God's truth, from the times of the Fathers, the Apostles and the martyrs."

"It is true, alas, it is true, that there are many sluggards, gluttons, profligates, and insolent beggars among monks."

"And yet how many meek and humble monks there are, yearning for solitude and fervent prayer in peace! These are less noticed or passed over in silence."

The most sacred place for the whole Orthodox world is Mount Athos [14]. It has 20 monasteries with 1500-2000 monks from different Orthodox countries: Greece, Bulgaria, Serbia, Romania, Russia, etc. The first monasteries were founded more than 1,000 years ago. There are no women on the island. Monks pray without ceasing all day from morning till night and even at night. The main purpose of their life is to get a place in Paradise through prayers, fasting and rituals. Everyone prays for his own salvation. It is a passive life attitude characteristic to the East thinking.

During the history, among the monks were both saints and sinners as was to be expected [15-18]. According to an article from the magazine Time [17] of April 28, 1941, "a large number of monks smoked, drank alcohol and even used drugs."

Athos church authorities have often collaborated with the powerful of the world. At different times, Athos was visited by the wealthy people of the Orthodox confession, who made great gifts [19]. Athos monasteries have a rich collection of well-preserved artifacts, rare books, ancient documents and works of art of great value.

The untold riches of Athos were endangered during the Second World War after the Nazi seizure of Greece.

Hitler sent his officials to make an inventory of the wealth of the monasteries. Then the executive committee of Athos, officially asked Hitler to put the autonomous monastic state under his personal protection, and Hitler happily agreed [16]. It was a great gift for Nazi propaganda in Orthodox countries. The monks of Athos called Adolf Hitler the "Great Patron of the Holy Mountain", his portraits were in the most honorable places. On the island were installed flags with a swastika.

14. ORTHODOX CHURCH IN RUSSIA

*I think the most important, most fundamental spiritual
need of the Russian people is the need for suffering,
everlasting and insatiable, everywhere and in everything.
... The Russian people are enjoying themselves with their
suffering.*

Fedor Mikhailovich Dostoevsky "Writer's diary"

The Russian Church is the largest ecclesiastically
independent Orthodox Church [20].

The religious authority in the Eastern Orthodox Church
is Patriarch. After him in the hierarchy of the church
follows Metropolitans, Archbishops and Bishops.

During the history the church officials closely
collaborated with the heads of state. Therefore, the exercise
of religion was strongly influenced by the state politics.

Grand Prince Vladimir of Kiev began the baptism in 998.
The Orthodoxy was made the national religion of the Slavic

state Kievan Rus.

In 1025, the Cathedral of Holy Wisdom (St. Sophia Cathedral), a copy of Constantinople Cathedral, was built in Kiev.

In the 11th century, Novgorod and several other principalities were baptized.

In 1237-40 the Mongols invaded and destroyed Kiev. After that, the residence of the Metropolitan of Kiev was in different years in Vladimir, Moscow, Smolensk and Vilnius.

In 1448 the Russian bishops elected their own Patriarch without recourse to Constantinople and the Russian church became independent (autocephalous).

In 1589 Job, Metropolitan of Moscow, was elevated to the post of patriarch with the approval of Constantinople.

In 1721, the patriarchate was abolished in Russia. The Moscow Diocese entered under the administration of the Most Holy Governing Synod.

Anointing of Ivan IV, the Terrible on the kingdom

One of the blackest pages of Moscow principality history is the reign of Ivan IV, the Terrible (1547 - 1584), which threw the development of the country back for several centuries.

In 1547, the prince of Moscow principality (or Moscovy)

Ivan IV was crowned as the Tsar.

Ivan methodically and carefully prepared everything for the coronation. He was crowned in the Assumption Cathedral. The order of Tsar anointing had a pronounced sacred character and included the sacrament - "an extraordinary gift of the Holy Spirit, communicated only to the prophets and the apostles". Thus, the Tsar was equated to a prophet or apostle.

The new name gave Ivan a new dimension of power, closely related to religion. Now he was a "divine" leader, appointed to receive God's will. The new title was then passed on from generation to generation, and subsequent Moscow rulers benefited from the divine nature of the power of the Russian monarch. Church and secular authorities are closely intertwined. The church preached that the will of God can manifest itself in the public life of the people only through the monarch.

In Kievan Rus, a completely different formula for correlation of secular and ecclesiastical authorities was adopted, corresponding to Justinian's sixth novel [21], in which the priesthood and kingdom are presented as two divine gifts, flowing from a single source, the interaction of which is only harmonious when everyone performs his inherent functions, that is, the church is spiritual, and the state is secular.

Unfortunately, the prescription of Justinian was

observed neither in the Byzantine Empire nor in Moscovy. In both cases, the church was a servant of state power.

In 1565, Ivan announced the introduction in the country of the Oprichnina - the state policy of terror. The oprichnics were Ivan's personal army and took the personal oath. The first victims of the oprichnina were the most prominent aristocrats. With the help of the guardsmen who were exempted from judicial responsibility, Ivan forcibly confiscated aristocrats' patrimonies. The decree on the introduction of the Oprichnina was approved by the supreme bodies of spiritual and secular authority - the Consecrated Council and the Aristocrat Assembly. The Orthodox Church in the Russian state ceased to be the be spiritual authority of the society and became the ministry of the tsar.

In 1569, having collected a huge army, Ivan went to Novgorod. Novgorod was the last stronghold of democracy left over from Kievan Rus [22]. In Novgorod, crafts flourished and there was a lively trade with the West, and there was going the Western style Reformation of the church. Ivan destroyed the Great Novgorod and most of the population of the city. With the destruction of the population, crafts which were usually passed on from one generation to another were destroyed, as well.

Ivan created a very special concept of royal power. He considered royal greatness equal to God's and therefore deprived his subjects of the right to discuss his actions.

Thus, Ivan destroyed the last ties with the democracy of Kievan Rus and with Europe. Recall that in Europe at that time there was already a later Renaissance, dozens of Universities were founded, and a church reform was in progress. Ivan created the vertical power of the Asian model of the Tatar-Mongol invasion. Moscovy lost any connection with Europe. From the very beginning to time of Peter I, Moscovy principality directed all its energy not to the development of the internal country life— education, crafts, commerce, etc., but to raids, wars, annexation and plunder.

Since that time, the Russian Orthodox Church, preaching and adhering to dogmas that have nothing to do with the teachings of Jesus Christ, has practically ceased to be Christian and has become an idol-worshiping religion. The Orthodox Church violated the covenants of Christ:

Render to Caesar the things that are Caesar's; and to God the things that are God's. (the church served only Caesar, knew little about the Christian creed and did not want to know)

-*Do not make yourself an idol* (the tsar was equated with God)

-*Love your neighbor as yourself.* (The priests blessed the troops in battle, the *commandment "do not kill" was not respected)*

- Do not steal, do not desire your neighbor's house; Do not desire your neighbor's wife, nor his slave, nor his slave, nor his ox, nor his ass, nothing that your neighbor has. (Oprichnics robbed, burned and killed in the name of the tsar, consecrated by the church).

At the time of Ivan IV in Moscovy there were priests and monks who called for the reform of the church. They were usually exiled to distant monasteries, and often executed. I will name a few: Maxim Greek, Matvey Bashkin, Theodosius Kosoy, and others. Their criticism was directed primarily against the external ceremonial side of the Orthodox religion. They considered ceremonies, such as the worship of icons and the holy cross, the sacraments, the veneration of relics, a special form of idolatry. "Do not come to the priests, do not create prayers, and do not demand their prayers, and do not repent, and do not take communion, and do not add thyme… - Theodosius Kosoy preached. He called the bishops "idol priests, false teachers."

The reformers preached that equality, fraternity and love of neighbor are the basic laws of Christianity. But what kind of equality and fraternity could be in the country of powerless slaves and the all-powerful king-robber with his servants?

In educational institutions for the preparation of clergy the future priests were taught that the content of the faith lay in the dogmas established by the fathers, and philosophy was applied primarily to clarify, substantiate and systematize the latter. Dogmas were strictly enforced.

Worship in the church was of a formal nature. Worship was a set of rituals, ceremonies and rites. The priests were little educated, as were their parishioners, and did not know the gospel. The Messenger to Muscovy, Marco Foscarino (1557), wrote about the numerous delusions of the people of the church, which stem from a lack of understanding of St. Scriptures.

Adam Olearius, a German philosopher and traveler, wrote on this subject: "... instruction in faith consists mainly in teaching to pray, honor the saints, make obeisance and the sign of the cross in front of their images."

The split of the Russian Orthodox Church

The split, Raskol, [23] occurred during the reign of the second tsar from the Romanov dynasty, Alexei I Mikhailovich (1629 -1676), father of Peter I. Alexei I, during the Russian-Polish war (1654-1667), visited several cities Vilna, Kovno, Grodno, Mogilev and others. Tsar liked the foreign life. From those countries, he brought new items of court furnishings: wallpaper, furniture of the German and Polish design, external carving in the Rococo style, etc.

But, unfortunately, he didn't bring Western ideas, for example, did not learn tolerance to dissenters.

Russian church rites, as Tsar remarked, differed from the western ones. The Ukrainian and Belarusian churches adhered to the Greek rite, while in Muscovy the old Constantinople rite was observed.

Tsar ordered Patriarch Nikon to reform the church. Nikon, not being too enlightened, decided that the differences in worship were due to the illiteracy of the Russian monks who were rewriting church books. In fact, the Greek and other churches gradually switched to new rites, and after the Turkish seizure of Greece, changes were made to the clothes of the priests reflecting Turkish fashion.

The reform took place in 1653-1655 and dealt with church rites and books. Three-finger baptism, belt bows instead of earthly ones, new-style clothing for worship, counterclockwise processions (formerly went clockwise) were introduced. Icons and church books were corrected according to Greek designs. Convened in 1654, the Moscovy Assembly approved the reform. Those who did not recognize the new rite were damned. Supporters of the old rites were declared dissenters and heretics.

Opponents of innovations were in all strata of Russian society, from the royal court to the peasants and from bishops to simple church officials. Many of them were executed or sent to distant monasteries.

The persecutions of Old Believers went throughout the Moscow kingdom. The refusal to accept reforms by the Solovki Monastery was perceived by the Moscow authorities as an open rebellion. Archers were sent. The Solovki monastery, which had been besieged several times since 1668, was taken in 1676. Almost all the 500 defenders of the monastery died in a short but hot fight. Only 60 people survived. The conquerors burned the monks with fire, drowned them in ice holes, hung them by hooks on the ribs, quartered them, and frozen them alive in ice [24].

Many people, mainly peasants, artisans and Cossacks fled to the northern and southern borders of the country, to Siberia, and even abroad, where they organized their own communities. Many dissenters fled to Belarus and Ukraine, where the Greek rite was held, but they were not prosecuted for their Old Believer worship. It was a mass exodus of ordinary Russian people who refused to follow the new church rituals.

The whole history of the split suggests that the Russian Orthodox Church was far from the teachings of Jesus Christ, who preached love of neighbor and non-use of violence. The Russian Orthodox Church was actually a pagan religion, where rituals were put at the head of the teachings. The church did not preach any moral values. The gospel was not among the main church books.

In the protests of the dissenters, the fanaticism of the Russian people was clearly manifested - the willingness to die for the faith, no matter whether it is reasonable or not.

During the peasant uprising for the reform of the church in Germany, the rebels demanded the reform of the church and a better life for themselves and their children. They called for more freedom, equality and for economic improvement. In Muscovy, dissenters demanded the observance of old rites, and many of them paid for it with their lives. How did the old worship improve their lives and the lives of their children? Why did they rebel? I think that changes in worship served as a pretext to pour out all the bitterness of their poor, powerless life. And there were many such riots, senseless and merciless in the history of the Russian people. They were brutally suppressed by royal power. Reasonable demands were not usually put forward by rebels. Such was the rebellion of Stepan Razin, where the rebels killed and robbed the evil landowners, but supported the rule of the tsar. With such idea, Pugachev's rebellion unfolded, and he led the rioters under the name of the murdered, but seemingly miraculous surviving Tsar Peter III. The church taught to pray for the Tsar - Father, and illiterate, poor, powerless people prayed.

Muscovy XVI-XVII centuries through the eyes of Europeans

The lack of rights of all segments of society was evidenced by Europeans who visited Moscovy.

The English Ambassador to Moscovy (1588) Giles Fletcher published the book "About the Russian Commonwealth" [25]. He wrote about the people of Moscovy:

"Seeing the rude and cruel acts with them of all the main officials and superiors, they also act inhumanly with each other, especially with lower ones. I often saw how merchants, having laid out their goods, all looked around and looked at the doors, like people who are afraid that they would be overtaken by some enemy. When I asked why they did this, I found out that they doubted whether any of the royal nobles' or the boyars' son was among the visitors. They could come with accomplices and take all goods by force".

Adam Olearius (1603-1671) [26], the German philosopher, scientist and traveler visited Muscovy four times. His books devoted to traveling around the country are one of the most remarkable literary phenomena of the seventeenth century, and at the same time, thanks to their accuracy, they are also one of the most important sources for studying the history of that time.

Olearius wrote about relations in Moscow society: "Their custom and disposition are such that they humiliate themselves before another person, bow down to noble people, down to the ground, and rushing to their feet. In their custom is thank for the beating and punishment. Just as all subjects, of high or low rank, are called royal serfs, the nobles have their slaves and serf workers and peasants. Princes and grandees are obliged to manifest slavery and insignificance before the king also in the fact that they must sign in letters and petitions with a diminutive name, that is, write "Ivashka", not "Ivan", "Petrushka, your serf", and not "Peter "".

Here is what Olearius [27-28] wrote about the church: "There is no doubt that their faith ... is Christian, but ... suspicious and in fact turns out to be very bad. Along with the Lord Christ, daily honor is also given to evangelicals, apostles, prophets and to many other saints and even written pictures that have to present these saints. ... In Moscow there is a special bargaining and shops where Russians sell such images or change them for money and silver. It is improper to say that you can buy gods.

The image is considered necessary for prayers by the Russians, and therefore they are not only in the church and with all the solemn church passages, but also at home, in the rooms, so that everyone can have an icon before their eyes during the prayer ...

The common people, especially those who live in villages, teach their children to the fear of God by putting them in front of images, forcing them in deep reverence and veneration to bow before them, to cross themselves and say: "Lord, have mercy!", However, it does not explain what the image means, so the children from an early age prefigure that the image is the essence of the gods, as they are usually called by the adults themselves.

There are also such Russians who, in a special pious mood, retire to the forests, and there, along the roads, build chapels in which they spend their harsh hermitage life and support themselves only with alms, which give them the peasants and the people passing by. We saw several such hermitage-dwellers on the way between Novgorod and Tver."

Augustin Meyerberg (1622 — 1688), Austrian baron, traveler and diplomat, ambassador to the Russian Tsar Alexei Mikhailovich (1661-63), author of "Journey to Muscovy" wrote:

"So, we were already in Moscow Russia, where the people are professing Jesus Christ only according to the Greek rite, ... they firmly hold on to this faith, into which, by the way, quite a few deviations from the Greek have crept in over time. ... Muscovites, though ignorant, even though they see nothing in the thick darkness of ignorance, are mostly ignorant of literacy, even though their faith is replete with obvious errors for common sense, but they still dare to brag that they are only Christians, but they called unclean all adherents of the Latin Church.

For the Roman High Priest, they still harbor such hatred, borrowed from the Greeks, that they never wanted to allow free worship to Catholics living in Moscow, while they easily give this freedom to Lutherans and Calvinists, knowing that they fell away from the Pope, although these people condemn the things that are highly respected among the Muscovites, such as: the image, the sign of the cross, and the invocation of the saints. "

Johann Korb (1672-1741) [30], the Austrian ambassador in Moscow during the time of the young Peter I left very detailed notes on the life and customs of the Muscovites. He wrote [31]:

"All the people of Moscow are more subject to slavery than they enjoy freedom, all Muscovites, whatever their rank, without the slightest respect for their personalities are under the yoke of the most severe slavery."

Rapprochement of Russia with Europe
Peter I the Great (1672-1725)

Peter I the Great made a long journey to the countries of Western Europe (1697-1698). Peter clearly realized the need for enlightenment in a dark, illiterate country and undertook a series of decisive measures. A school of mathematical and navigation sciences, and artillery, engineering and medical schools were opened in Moscow. The engineering school and the maritime academy in St. Petersburg, and the mining schools at the Olonets and Ural factories were established. The goals of mass education were to open arithmetic schools in provincial cities, where tuition was supposed to be free. A network of theological schools was created for the training of priests. Peter's decrees introduced compulsory education for noblemen and clergy, since even they were mostly illiterate. Thus, in the reign of Peter the foundation was laid for the spread of education in Russia.

Russian language has been enriched with thousands of new words needed in science, engineering, maritime affairs, etc., borrowed from European languages. The Academy of Sciences, founded by Peter, was opened a few months after his death. Peter invited foreign scientists, architects and artists to Russia and at the same time sent talented young people to study abroad.

Historian Klyuchevsky tells [32] how difficult it was for Peter to achieve success in this field. Pupils sent abroad often did not study there. The noble children ran away from school, so the mixed schools were organized, and the poor children received scholarships [33].

Peter issued a decree, in which people were instructed to write names in petitions and other documents completely instead of derogatory semi-names (Ivashka, Senka, etc.), do not fall on their knees in front of the tsar, in winter in the cold do not take off their hats. He explained the need for these innovations in such a way: "Less baseness, more zeal for service and loyalty to me and the state,"

Peter gave a new name to his state: the Russian Empire. This name was adopted by Europe and the country was no longer called Muscovy, but Russia.

Strengthening autocracy, Peter strengthened slavery even more. Like his predecessors, Peter constantly waged wars and invented more and more new taxes, robbed his own people. The people received nothing from conquests, although they paid for them in blood.

Historian V. Klyuchevsky wrote: "Peter did not touch the foundations of a public warehouse, enshrined in the Code, neither class division by type of service, nor serfdom. On the contrary, he complicated old class duties with new ones. ... Peter increased the income budget three times as much. ... The war, with its consequences, intercepted all the surpluses of national earnings ... The people of labor generation, who went to Peter, did not work for itself, but to the state and, after intensive and improved work, was almost poorer than generation of their fathers ... So, Peter took from the old Russia supreme state power, law, estates, and from the West borrowed technical means for the organization of the army, fleet, state and national economy, government institutions ... Peter's reform was a struggle of despotism with the people, with its inertia. He hoped with a terror of power to cause activity in the enslaved society and through the slave-owning nobility to establish European science in Russia ... He wanted the slave, while remaining a slave, to act consciously and freely."

Pushkin's words about Peter that he "cut a window to Europe". characterize the Peter's deeds accurately. He didn't widely open the door to Europe, but only cut through a window. European ideas could, through this open window, illuminate the life of the Russian elite, introducing it to European culture. "Faith in the miraculous power of education, which penetrated Peter, his awesome cult of science forcibly ignited a spark of enlightenment in slave minds, which gradually burst into a meaningful striving for truth, that is, for freedom," wrote Klyuchevsky.

Russia after Peter I

As for the people, many of Peter's undertakings were forgotten or banned by subsequent rulers. Estate schools, in which children of different social classes could study, were closed. Some of the arithmetic schools were turned into schools for Orthodox priests. But the level of illiteracy of the noble society quickly fell, since it became fashionable to hire foreigners as home teachers. They gave children primary education and taught them languages and European manners. Later Russian teachers emerged.

Peter's intentions included mostly pragmatic training — the sciences needed to strengthen the army and government: mathematical, artillery and navigation, legal and economic knowledge. Successes in these sciences required labor, to which the Russian nobility was not accustomed. They already earned income from their serfs without any effort.

Subsequent Russian rulers mostly led Russia along its beaten path — intensifying autocracy, war, robbery, and even more enslaving the peasants.

But gradually and slowly, writers, poets, philosophers, etc., began to appear in Russia.

"By streamlining and strengthening noble land tenure and soul ownership, legislation strengthened the serfdom. The landlord's judicial and police power were enriched by a decree of May 6, 1736, which allowed to determine the punishment of a serf for escaping. The decree of May 2, 1758 obliged, more precisely, empowered the landowner to observe the behavior of his serfs. Finally, the decree of December 13, 1760 gave the right to landowners to exile serfs to Siberia for settlement, set off by recruits." At the same time, the law increasingly depersonalized the serf, erasing the last signs of a competent person. The landowner traded in them as a living commodity, not only selling them without land to people of any rank, but also tearing them away from the family. " - wrote Klyuchevsky.

The next push after Peter, which led to the rapprochement of Russia with Europe, was made by the war of 1812 with Napoleon. After Russia won the war, the Russian army passed through all Europe and in 1814, together with its allies, triumphantly entered Paris. Russian soldiers and officers could compare the free seething life of European countries with the sleepy, disenfranchised, illiterate, roadless, slowly developing life of the Russian people. This led to the Decembrist uprising and to the wide participation of the Russian intelligentsia in discussions of issues related to the future of Russia and its people and ways that could lead Russia to Europe and change the Eastern values for Western ones.

I wrote about these ideas in detail in the blog "Social, philosophical and political ideas of Russia in the 19th century" [34].

While at the beginning of the 18th century the French populace from the poorer strata immigrated to Russia, looking for easy, well-paid jobs, at the end of the 18th century, during the French Revolution, a wave of immigration brought French nobility and royalists, many of whom were Catholic. They brought the Gospel in French.

Thus, the Gospel became available to almost all educated nobles. Some of them began to convert to Catholicism.

Pushkin wrote (1836):

"There is a book, by which every word is interpreted, explained, preached in all corners of the earth, applied to all sorts of circumstances of the world and the events of the world; from which you cannot repeat a single expression that everyone would not know by heart, which would not be the proverb of the nations; It does not conclude anything unknown to us, but this book is called the Gospel - and such is its everlasting beauty, that if we, fed up with the world or depressed by despondency, accidentally open it, then we are no longer able to resist her sweet passion and immerse spirit in her divine eloquence. "

Pushkin most probably read the Gospel in French in 1836, long before the Gospel was translated into Russian.

The Bible was translated into Russian only in the second half of the nineteenth century. In 1815 Alexander I ordered to translate the Gospel into Russian, but the church did not hurry with the translation. In 1858, Alexander II authorized the translation of the Bible. In 1863, the Russian-language New Testament and in 1876 the entire Bible saw the light [35].

In order to resist the spread of new ideas and preserve autocracy, under Nicholas I, intensive propaganda of Orthodoxy, autocracy and nationality began. The Minister of Public Education, Count Uvarov, presented to Nikolay I the doctrine to which all Russian education was to follow.

Uvarov said that the Russian nation is an association of people boundlessly loyal to their rulers, that humility is a special feature of the Russian nation, and Western nations are corrupted by Enlightenment philosophy. The "nationality" was a form of state patriotism and was interpreted as a commitment of the masses to the "originally Russian principles" - autocracy and Orthodoxy. The idea parasitized on the darkness, the downtrodden and pagan religiosity of the peasantry. The unification of the tsar with the people leads to a conflict-free existence of society, to stability, Uvarov argued.

Nicholas I believed that the tsar and the state is the same thing. The Police Spy Third Division looked after everyone, there was no exception for anyone, so the Tsar seemed omnipresent and all-powerful.

Uvarov was right in asserting that humility is a special feature of the Russian nation. All foreigners who visited Muscovy and Russia spoke about this feature of the Russian people.

In 1839, Nicholas I invited the French Monarchist Marquis de Custine to visit Russia and write a book about it. After visiting Russia, de Custine became a Republican. Quotes from the book "Russia in 1839" [36]:

"On the Russian border, every stranger is treated as an accused."

"Where there is no freedom, there is no soul and truth"

"In Russia, conversation is equal to conspiracy, thought is equal to rebellion."

"A peasant living near Paris is far freer than a landowner in Russia."

"The emperor is the only person in Russia who can talk to without fear of snitches."

"Russia is a terrifying combination of the European mind and science with the spirit of Asia"

"For all its immensity, this empire is nothing but a prison, the key of which is in the hands of the emperor."

"Oppression cannot exist without universal silence."

"In Russia, despotism is on the throne, but tyranny is everywhere."

"In Petersburg, to lie is to fulfill your civic duty"

"Everybody here is spying, even if amateur and free of charge."

"No matter how hard you try, Muscovy will always remain a country more Asian than European."

Speaking about religion in Russia, de Custine noted: "In Orthodox churches, sermons have always occupied a very modest place. In Russia, the spiritual and secular authorities vigorously opposed theological disputes. As soon as there was a desire to discuss issues that divided Rome and

Byzantium, both sides were ordered to silence. In essence, the subjects of the dispute are so insignificant that a split continues to exist only due to ignorance in religious matters. Some theological schools teach some theological subjects, but they only tolerated and are sometimes prohibited. The fact will seem completely incomprehensible and inexplicable to you, but, nevertheless, it is so - the Russian people do not teach religion."

Peter Chaadaev (1794-1856) on East and West

Of the Russian philosophers, Chaadaev most deeply understood the problems of stagnation in Russian society and the slavish obedience of the Russian people.

Chaadaev was born in an old wealthy noble family. In 1807–1811 he attended lectures at Moscow University, was friends with the writer A. Griboedov and the future Decembrists N.I. Turgenev and I.D. Yakushkin. During the Patriotic War of 1812 he participated in the Battle of Borodino, went to bayonet attack at Kulm, was awarded the Russian Order of St. Anne and the Prussian Cross of Kulma. He participated in the battle of Tarutino, at Maloyaroslavets, Lutzen, Bautzen, near Leipzig, went to Paris. Traveled to Europe (1923-1926). In 1829-1831 he created his famous "Philosophical Letters" [37]. The publication in the journal of the first letter caused a strong discontent of the authorities because of the bitter indignation expressed in it about the separation of Russia from the "global education of the human race", spiritual stagnation. The journal was closed, and Chaadaev was declared a Madman.

Chaadaev wrote:

"The world was originally divided into two parts - East and West. This is not only geographical division, but also the order of things, due to the very nature of the rational being: these are two principles corresponding to the two dynamic forces of nature, two ideas embracing the whole life structure of the human race. Concentrating, deepening, becoming locked in oneself, the human mind was built up in the East; scattering outward, radiating in all directions, struggling with all obstacles, it develops in the West. "

"The first was the East and poured out on the earth streams of light from the depths of his solitary contemplation; then the West came with its all-encompassing activity, its living word and omnipotent analysis, mastered its works, finished the East, and finally absorbed it in its wide girth. But in the East, submissive minds, kneeling before historical authority, were exhausted in uncomplaining service to the sacred principle for them and eventually fell asleep, locked in their fixed synthesis, not knowing the new destinies that were prepared for them;

meanwhile, in the West, they walked proudly and freely, bowing only before the authority of mind and heaven, stopping only before the unknown, constantly gazing into the boundless future. And here they are still going forward - you know it, and you know also that from the time of Peter the Great and we thought we were going along with them."

"But here is a new school. No longer need the West, it is necessary to destroy the creation of Peter the Great, we must again go into the desert. Forgetting what the West has done for us, not knowing gratitude to the great man who civilized us, and to Europe that taught us, they reject Europe and the great man, and in the heat of passion this newly made patriotism is already in a hurry to declare us loved children of the East, ... we have a real revolution in national thought, a passionate reaction against enlightenment, against the ideas of the West."

"We live in the east of Europe - this is true, and yet we never belonged to the East. The East has its own history, which has nothing in common with ours. It has, as we just saw, a fruitful idea that at one time led to the enormous development of the mind, which fulfilled its purpose with amazing power, but which was no longer destined to reappear on the world stage. "

We saw, after the reforms of Peter I, Russia was divided into two unequal parts: on the one hand, educated nobility and aristocracy, who learn from the West and often imitated it, and on the other hand, a huge number of dark, illiterate, disenfranchised slaves, with the remained from the Tatar invasion Asian habits, rites, customs and conventions, and with Orthodoxy - the religion, which had little to do with Christianity. For many centuries of unfreedom, humiliation, poverty and lawlessness, the Russian people accepted suffering as a way of life. Dostoevsky wrote: "I think the most important, most fundamental spiritual need of the Russian people is the need for suffering, everlasting and insatiable, everywhere and in everything. ... The Russian people enjoy their suffering, as it were." (Writer's diary)

Church and Peasant Reform 1861

The official church did not approve the manifesto of the peasant emancipation in 1861. Since the end of 1857, Metropolitan Filaret has been actively involved in public work to prepare the Peasant Reform. He pointed to the obligation [39] "according to the Christian law for every soul to obey the powers."

"The question of the peasants is dark, controversial, unresolved, not allowing us to foresee what the solution will be. ... We have a duty to maintain loyalty and devotion in our subjects to the most pious sovereign; for this purpose it is proper to say in a sermon that he cares about the elevation and well-being of all classes, not excluding the lower ones, but it's not our business to enter into controversial details, and it may happen that we do not guess the thoughts of the government, not yet open, and in this case, let us go down in vain with the church road, on the political road to stumble into a hole," wrote dodgy Filaret to Alexis, Archbishop of Tver.

Slavophile Prince Cherkassky, who also participated in the preparation of the reform, wrote in the article "Some features of the future rural management" [39]: "The basis of the thought about the non-humiliation of the slave state and the non-shame of corporal punishment (in itself) is in the Russian people the idea of religion, expressed in popular sayings:: Lord ordered the slaves to serve faithfully to their masters or the Lord suffered and told us to. These sayings are based on the parables of the Lord about slaves and talents and on the passions of Christ; the Russian man cannot allow that the punishment suffered by the Savior to be humiliating for a man; Of all the evidence presented, it can be seen that the serfdom does not insult the Russian person and that in a moral sense it is not as humiliating in Russia as it seems for foreigners or people with foreign notions." He proposed that the landowner be granted the right to corporal punishment of peasants (up to 18 hits by sticks).

Metropolitan Filaret agreed that "the serfdom does not offend the Russian people" and that "in a moral sense it is not so humiliating in Russia as it seems for foreigners or people with foreign concepts."

"... the closest police oversight of the peasantry is necessary for their own moral development and is useful for the productivity of the state in general," Filaret said. Note that for the moral development of the peasants, "the closest police oversight" is needed, and not the teaching of Jesus Christ of love of neighbor.

"The extensive Christian catechism of the Orthodox Church"[40] for the use of all Orthodox Christians, published under Filaret, according to "His Imperial Majesty's highest command" said: "It is not a lawless murder ... when the enemy is killed in the war for the Sovereign and the fatherland", in other words the commandment "Thou shalt not kill" was not necessary to be observed.

Protestant denominations in Russia in the second half of the XIX century

The Gospel in Russian language was published in 1863, and, as the Moscow Metropolitan Filaret predicted, this brought a lot of anxiety and trouble to the Orthodox Church. Protestant denominations began to spread, preaching the teachings of Christ by the gospel and rejecting the ideas, customs and rituals of the Orthodox

Church. In Russia, they were called sects, banned and persecuted. Among the Protestant sects in Russia were Baptists, Evangelicals, Lutherans, Dukhobors (corresponding to the Quakers), Pentecostals, Mennonites and many others.

The Russian Protestant movement, Tolstoism, appeared and spread. Its founder was Count Leo Tolstoy, a writer, the author of "War and peace", a great thinker, and a patriot (not in the official sense of the word).

In 1881 Tolstoy wrote Confession [41]. In this work, Tolstoy describes his path from Orthodoxy to the true Christian faith.

"Despite ... doubts and suffering, I still held on to Orthodoxy. But there were questions of life that had to be resolved, and then the resolution of these issues by the church - contrary to the very foundations of the faith that I lived - finally made me renounce the possibility of communication with Orthodoxy. These questions were, firstly, the attitude of the Orthodox Church to other churches - towards Catholicism and towards the so-called dissenters. At this time, due to my interest in the faith, I became close to the believers of different confessions: Catholics, Protestants, Old Believers, Molokans, etc. And I met a lot of people morally high and truly believers. I wanted to be a brother of these people. And what? The teaching that promised me to unite everyone by faith and love is the very teaching in their best Representatives told me that these people are in a lie, that what gives them the power of life is the temptation of the devil and that we are alone in possession of the only possible truth.

... The second attitude of the church to life issues was its attitude to war and executions.

At this time there was a war in Russia. And the Russians began to kill their brothers in the name of Christian love. It was impossible not to think about it. It was impossible not to see that killing is evil, offensive to the very first fundamentals of all faith. And at the same time in the churches they prayed for the success of our weapons, and the teachers of the faith recognized this murder as a matter arising from faith. And not only these killings in the war, but during those disturbances that followed the war, I saw members of the church, its teachers, monks, schemas, who approved the killing of the lost helpless youths. And I paid attention to everything that is being done by people professing Christianity, and I was horrified. "

In 1884 Tolstoy wrote "What is my faith?" [42]

Tolstoy rejects the tenets of the organized church, but highly espouses the moral principles of Christianity. The main principles are forgiveness, non-resistance to evil by violence, rejection of hostility with any people, "love of neighbor", moral self-help, simplicity and primacy of spiritual values over material.

"The rules given by the church about faith in dogmas, about the observance of sacraments, fasting, prayers, I did not need; and the rules based on Christian truths, did not exist. Moreover, the church rules weakened, sometimes directly destroyed the Christian mood, which alone gave me the meaning of my life. Most of all I was embarrassed by the fact that all human evil - condemnation of private people, condemnation of whole nations, condemnation of other faiths and arising from such condemnations: execution, war, all this was justified by the church. The teaching of Christ about humility, non-condemnation, forgiveness of offenses, self-denial and love in words was magnified by the church, and at the same time that was approved in practice was incompatible with this teaching.

... The Christian (Orthodox) church from the time of Constantine did not demand any actions from its members. It did not even declare any demands for abstention from anything. The Christian church recognized and sanctified all that was in the pagan world. She recognized and sanctified both divorce, and slavery, and the courts, and all those authorities that had being, and wars, and executions ... The Church, in words recognizing the teachings of Christ, in life directly denied them.

And I was convinced that the church doctrine, despite the fact that it called itself Christian, is the very darkness against which Christ fought and ordered his disciples to fight.

But the time has come and the light of the true doctrine of Christ, which was in the Gospels, despite the fact that the church, feeling its untruth, tried to hide it (forbidding Bible translations), the time has come, and this light through so-called sectarians, even through free-thinkers of the world penetrated the people, and the infidelity of the church teaching became obvious to people, and they began to change their former life, by virtue of the teachings of Christ that had come down to them."

In 1901 the Holy Synod excommunicated Tolstoy from the church. In essence, Tolstoy was excommunicated for preaching the gospel — the teachings of Jesus Christ.

In response to the Synod, Tolstoy wrote: "No matter how anyone understands the person of Christ, his teaching, which destroys the evil of the world, is so simple, easy, surely gives good to people, unless they pervert it. This teaching is hidden, everything is redone in the rude witchcraft of bathing, smearing with oil, body movements, spells, swallowing pieces, etc., so that nothing remains of the teaching. And if when a person tries to remind people that the teachings of Christ are not in these wizards, not in prayers, mass, candles, icons but that people love each other, did not pay evil for evil, did not judge, did not kill each other, then a moan of indignation will rise from those who benefit from these deceptions, and these people publicly, with incomprehensible audacity speak in churches, printed in books, newspapers, catechisms, that Christ never forbade an oath (swear), never forbade murder (execution, war), that the doctrine of nonresistance to evil with satanic cunning was invented by the enemies of Christ.

I believe in the following: I believe in God, whom I understand as spirit, as love, as the beginning of everything. I believe that he is in me and I in him. I believe that the will of God is more clearly, more apprehensible expressed in the teachings of the man Christ. In my opinion it is the greatest blasphemy to assume that Christ is God and pray to him. I believe that the true good of man is in the fulfillment of the will of God, and his will is that people love each other and, as a result, would do to others the way they want to do to them, as stated in the Gospel, this is the whole law and the prophets.

I went the opposite way. I began by saying that I loved my Orthodox faith more than my peace of mind, then I loved Christianity more than my church, but now I love the truth more than anything in the world. And so far, the truth coincides for me with Christianity, as I understand it. And I confess this Christianity; and to the extent that I confess it, I live peacefully and joyfully and calmly and joyfully approach death. "

"The real faith is not to know which days are lean, which ones to go to the temple and which to listen to and read prayers, but to always live a good life in love with everyone, always deal with your neighbors as you wish to come with you. " ("The Way of Life")

The works of Tolstoy in the 1880s and 1890s were banned in Russia by censorship and first published abroad, in Russian or in translation. The forbidden works of Tolstoy were published in Russia after the adoption of the law on tolerance in 1905.

The spread of Tolstoy's ideas in Russia began during the 1890s. The movement continued to grow after the writer's death and was strong in the years immediately after the 1917 revolution with agricultural communities established in the provinces of Smolensk, Tver, Samara, Kursk, Perm and Kiev. Tolstoy communities were destroyed in the late 1920s, when collectivization began, and Tolstoian leaders were sent to the Gulag.

The ideas of non-violent resistance, expounded by Leo Tolstoy in his work "The Kingdom of God Within You," influenced Mahatma Gandhi [43], who corresponded with Russian writer, Martin Luther King and others.

Religion in the USSR and the Russian Federation

After the October 1917 coup, the Bolsheviks began the eradication of religion as incompatible with Marxist ideology. They immediately began to rob the church. The decree "On Land" [44] of 1917 nationalized the monastery and church lands "with all their living and dead implements, manor buildings and all accessories". Since November 1917, state funding for religious schools has ceased. On February 5, 1918, the Bolsheviks adopted the "Decree on the separation of church from state and school from church" [45], which consolidated the secular nature of the state and authorized the seizure of church property and the termination of payments to the clergy. The decree deprived religious organizations of the rights of legal entities and property rights. All buildings that previously belonged to religious organizations, became the property of the state. Monks and clergymen of churches and religious cults were deprived of voting rights.

In addition to the propaganda of atheism, government bodies in the 1920s-1930s carried out mass arrests and harassment of clergy and religious preachers. Up until 1939, the policy of eliminating organized religious life was administratively carried out by state authorities, in particular the NKVD (the interior ministry of the Soviet Union).

In 1922 the Bolsheviks launched a large-scale campaign to seize church property. Icons, art objects, cult objects made of precious metals, and even "koltezhtsy" — boxes in which the relics of the saints were kept — were seized. The boxes were often made of precious metals, some of which were objects of jewelry. They were taken away, and the relics were thrown away or handed over to museums.

On March 19, 1922, Lenin wrote to members of the Political Bureau of the Central Committee of the Party (strictly secret):

"We need to carry out the removal of church valuables in the most decisive and quickest way, by which we can secure a fund of several hundred million gold rubles (we must recall the enormous wealth of some monasteries and laurel) ... The greater the number of representatives of the reactionary clergy and the reactionary bourgeoisie we will succeed to shot on this occasion, the better."

Between 1917 and 1935, 130,000 Orthodox priests were arrested. Of these, 95,000 were put to death.

Patriarch Tikhon (1865-1925) [46] first wrote protests about Bolshevik politics. In January 19, 1918 Tikhon issued his famous Appeal, which, in particular, read: "Come to your senses, madmen, stop your bloody reprisals. After all, what you are doing is not only a cruel thing, it is truly a satanic cause for which you are subject to hell fire in the future life - the afterlife and terrible curse of posterity in the life on this earth."

The second protest was the Appeal to the Council of People's Commissars of October 13/26, 1918: "All who take the sword will perish by the sword" (Matthew 26:52)

"In truth, you gave them (the people) a stone instead of bread and a snake instead of fish (Matthew 7: 9-10). To the people, worn out by a bloody war, you promised to give peace "without annexations and indemnities." ... Instead of annexations and indemnities, our great homeland was conquered, diminished, dismembered and in return for paying the tribute imposed on it, you secretly export gold to Germany. "

He was persecuted, arrested, interrogated. From August 1922 to the spring of 1923, the Patriarch was regularly interrogated. In April 1923, at a meeting of the Politburo of the Central Committee of the RCP (B), a secret resolution was adopted, according to which the Tribunal was to give Saint Tikhon the death sentence. In the Soviet press in the spring of 1923, letters were published from citizens who demanded to severely punish "cannibal Tikhon".

Before trial on June 16, 1923, Tikhon wrote repentance. "When addressing this statement to the Supreme Court of the RSFSR, I consider it necessary, on the duty of my pastoral conscience, to state the following:

"Being raised in a monarchical society and being under the influence of anti-Soviet people until my arrest, I was really hostile to Soviet power, and the hostility from a passive state at times shifted to active actions. Recognizing the correctness of the Court's decision to prosecute me for the anti-Soviet activities of the criminal code in the indictment, I repent of these misconducts against the state system and ask the Supreme Court to change my preventive measure, that is, to release me from custody.

At the same time, I declare to the Supreme Court that from now on the Soviet power is not the enemy. I finally and decisively dissociate myself from both the foreign and the internal monarchical-White Guard counterrevolution".

On March 13, 1924, the investigation of the case against Patriarch Tikhon was terminated by a decision of the Political Bureau of the Central Committee of the RCP (B), But he was continued to be arrested and interrogated until his death on April 7, 1925.

On March 11, 1931, the Bible was outlawed in the USSR, imposing a ban not only on its publication, but also on sale and import from other countries. The Bible in the USSR remained a banned book, for the distribution and even storage for which you could go to prison. Only after the solemn celebration of the 1000th anniversary of the Baptism of Russia in June 1988, this ban was secretly lifted.

The Patriarch is elected by the Synod. Before the convocation of the Synod, the position of patriarch is performed by locum tenens. After Tikhon, the locum tenens became Metropolitan Peter (Polansky) [47]. Metropolitan Peter was arrested in November 1925, and his deputy, Metropolitan Sergius (Stragorodsky) (1867- 1944), declared himself the locum tenens [48].

From this moment the church governance faithfully served the communist power.

On July 29, 1927, Metropolitan Sergius issued the Message "On the attitude of the Orthodox Russian Church to the existing civil authority":

"We want to be Orthodox and at the same time recognize the Soviet Union as our civic homeland, whose joys and successes are our joys and successes, and failures our failures. ... We will publicly express our gratitude to the Soviet Government for such attention to the spiritual needs of the Orthodox population, and at the same time we assure the Government that we will not use the trust placed in us for evil deeds."

In connection with this message, the term Sergionism appeared, denoting a policy of unconditional loyalty to the Soviet power. It must be said that at this time the Bolsheviks arrested and shot many Orthodox clerics.

With the beginning of the war, Sergius get the opportunity to preach hatred for enemies and bless Russian soldiers to the manslaughter, as Orthodox church ministers did before him for many centuries.

On November 24, 1941, Metropolitan Sergius and Metropolitan Nicholas released the first message in the evacuation to the flock: "Hitler's Moloch continues to broadcast to the world as if he had raised his sword for "defense of religion and salvation" of the allegedly desecrated faith. But the whole world knows that the false guise of piety only covers its atrocities. In all the countries enslaved by him, he creates vile abuse of freedom of conscience, mocks shrines, destroys the temples of God, imprisons and executes Christian shepherds, pushes in prisons believers who rebel against his insane pride, against his plans to establish his satanic power over the Earth. The Orthodox, who had escaped from fascist captivity, told us about the mockery of the fascists over the temples. "

It was a blatant lie and propaganda. In the territories occupied by the Germans, churches were restored and opened up for sacred service. During the counteroffensive of the Red Army near Moscow in December 1941, the temples, restored during the short period of occupation of the territory of the Moscow and Tula regions, were closed, and the priests who served in them were subjected to repression.

Stalin liked consistent political loyalty to the communist regime, manifested by the leadership of the Moscow

Patriarchate in the first six months of the war, and its vigorous fundraising activities for defense. On September 4, 1943, the historical meeting of Stalin with Metropolitan Sergius and Metropolitans Alexi and Nikolai took place.

Stalin, briefly noting the positive significance of the patriotic activity of the church during the war, asked Metropolitans Sergius, Alexi, and Nicholas to comment on the questions of the Patriarchate and their own urgent, but unresolved issues.

Metropolitan Sergius told Stalin that the most important ... issue is the question of the central leadership of the Church ... and therefore he considers it desirable that the Government allow the Bishops' Council to be assembled, who elect the patriarch, and also form the Holy Synod as the head of the church, a deliberative body of 5–6 hierarchs. The most important issue for Sergius was his election as patriarch, although there was going a war and the people, and the church had more vital problems. Sergius was elected patriarch after 4 days, on September 8.

The issues of the opening of churches in a number of dioceses and the organization of theological courses were also discussed. The opening of the seminaries and the Academy proposed by Stalin, the metropolitans rejected. There, it was necessary to teach the gospel, to talk about morality. The metropolitans said that there was enough to held theological courses, where students were taught the rituals of the church service: to say prayers, wave the censer, make bows to the earth, and also know the rites of baptism, wedding and burial.

Stalin ordered the addition of metropolitans to the nomenclature, privileged upper communist elite. The metropolitans received a 3-storey mansion with all the property, furniture, available in this mansion, which was occupied by the formerly German ambassador Schulenburg. Stalin added that the metropolitans will be provided with products at state (non-market) prices and will be provided with 2–3 passenger cars with fuel." In conclusion of this reception, Metropolitan Sergius made a thank-you address to the Government and personally to Comrade Stalin.

On October 27, 1943, Patriarch Sergius handed over a statement asking for the release of 24 bishops, 1 archimandrite and 1 archpriest who were in Soviet camps. However, all but one of the clergymen mentioned in the list were either shot or died in the camps by this time.

In the first months of the war, the Russian Orthodox Church began to carry out activities related to collecting money and other material assets from the congregation which were transferred to the defense fund. By the end of the war, the Russian Orthodox Church raised more than 300 million rubles, not counting jewels and products. In most cases, material assistance was provided to the Red Army.

The transfer of the Dmitry Donskoi tank column to the Red Army by the funds of the Russian Orthodox Church, which had 40 tanks, was widely reported in the Soviet mass media in 1944. At that time there were hungry children in the country, old men and women, there were wounded people in need of help, but the Orthodox Church was spending the money raised by the people on tanks. The commandments "Thou shalt not kill," and "love your neighbor" were not important for the Church officials. Much more important was the favor of the new ruler, Comrade Stalin, because he decided whom to execute, and whom to award, and also approved the nomenclature lists.

During the N. S. Khrushchev rule the persecution of the believers, the destruction of churches and atheistic hysteria in the media began again. Zealous Komsomol members stayed at the church fences, taking "notes" of all who came to the service.

The persecutions of the Church and believers continued for many years after Khrushchev.

In Perestroika, there is a gradual revision of the state policy towards the church. Perestroika provided everyone with the opportunity to purchase the gospel book.

During these years of great changes in the relations of church and state, Alexi II was the patriarch of Moscow and All Russia, in the world Alexey Mikhailovich Rydiger

(1990-2008) [49]. Several laws were passed, giving the church the rights that it had before the revolution.

In 1990, a law was passed that approved the rights of a legal entity to individual parishes, church institutions and the Patriarchate.

In 1997, a new law "On Freedom of Conscience and Religious Associations" was adopted. The law recognized the historical role of the Orthodox Church in the fate of Russia. The provision on the separation of the school from the Church was formulated in such a way that allowed the teaching of creed in general educational schools on an optional basis.

In November 2004, amendments were made to the Tax Code of the Russian Federation, exempting religious organizations from paying land tax.

At all times, the priests were required to cooperate with the KGB. Some did it to a minimum, others did what was required of them, and still others did everything it takes for the sake of a career.

December 5, 2008, on the day of the death of Patriarch Alexi II, the BBC wrote [49], summarizing his episcopal career:

"Patriarch Alexi II had an incredible career, during which he switched from suppressing the Russian Orthodox Church to be its champion. A favorite of the KGB, he quickly moved into the church hierarchy, following instructions from the Kremlin at a time when dissident priests were thrown into prison. As the de facto foreign minister of the Church, he helped hide repression against Russian Christians, defending the Soviet system in front of the outside world. He quickly rose and was elected head of the Russian Orthodox Church at a key moment in 1990, when the USSR was approaching its collapse. Surprisingly, it is quite likely that he took advantage of the moment and became the head of the revival and prosperity of the Church."

The current patriarch Cyril (Vladimir Mikhailovich Gundyaev) [50-54] graduated from the Leningrad Theological Academy in 1970. In 1969 he was tonsured a monk with the name Cyril. Cyril began to quickly climb the corporate ladder, each year climbing up more and more stairs. February 1, 2009 Kirill was elected patriarch.

He faithfully served the KGB, where he had the nickname Mikhailov. Cyril is a billionaire [51-52], who made a state on duty-free importation of alcohol and cigarettes. He is a Putin's friend who fights against human rights and against Western Christian values - freedom, tolerance, love of neighbor, non-resistance to evil by violence [53]. Cyril defends the nationalist concept of the "Russian world". Patriarch Cyril stated that the Russian war in Syria is a "holy war" [54]. The sermons of Patriarch

Kirill are far from the Gospel, from the ideas preached by Christ. Cyril can't be called a Christian

Currently, the Orthodox Church preaches the same ideas that she had been preaching for centuries. In June 2015, Archpriest Chaplin predicted a quick war to society and explained that it is the norm. "The peace does not usually live for long. The peace now, thank God, will not be long either. Why do I say, "thank God"? A society in which there is too much well-fed, calm, trouble-free and comfortable life is a society left by God. Such a society does not live for a long time", said the archpriest in the program "Special Opinion" on Echo of Moscow [55].

Only atheism was permitted in the USSR. The school taught that believing in God is a sign of backwardness and lack of culture. Therefore, several generations of atheists have grown up. Many of the Russian atheists, although they now go to church, because it is fashionable, have become pagans, since this is the most primitive, initial level of human faith, which practically does not require knowledge and mental effort. The survey conducted among Muscovites by the center of Moscow State University showed that Orthodox Christians who believe in horoscopes are 26%, in witchcraft damage and bad eye - 47% in Spiritualism - 18%". Authors found comparing the consciousness of definitely believers and definitely non-believers (atheists), "that atheists are 2-4 times less susceptible to superstition, occultism, and satanism then believers. Thus, the ratio of believers in witchcraft among Christian believers and atheists is 57% and 21%, in astrology - 29% and 15%, in spiritualism - 25% and 6%, respectively," [56]

Russia is the richest country in natural resources, but its population is one of the poorest in Europe, with almost 20 million people living below the poverty line. Corruption, theft, drunkenness, drugs, homeless children, vagrants, very high men's mortality, poverty, poor schools, bad medicine are common and accepted.

Muscovy Principality began its history as a Christian country, but over time, the Orthodox Church went far from Christian teaching and became a servant of the rich and powerful. After the translation of the New Testament into Russian in the second half of the 19th century, the movement of the Reformation began in Russia, almost 4 centuries late compared with Europe. It was interrupted by the seizure of power by the Communists who persecuted all religions. The communist teaching was based on the belief that the main goal of humanity is material well-being, and any means can be used to achieve the goal. ("End justifies the means"). Hate was preached to the bourgeoisie, the priests, the intelligentsia, to all who could be robbed, and to all those who disagreed with the communist ideology. Robberies, denunciations, murders, the Gulag, enslavement of the peasants, famines, propaganda, turning the truth inside out, etc. were used as means. Time passed and promised by the Communists material well-being was not achieved. The Soviet Union fell, leaving behind the backwardness, corruption and low moral level of the upper classes, including the leadership of the Orthodox Church.

It is necessary to continue the reform of the church, which was interrupted in 1917.

Russia should strive for Europe with its Christian values: equality and respect for human dignity.

15. EAST AND WEST
HORIZONTAL AND VERTICAL RELATIONSHIPS IN SOCIETY

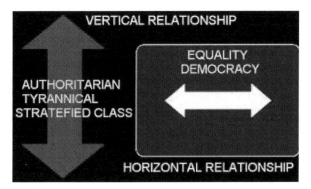

Horizontal and vertical relationships in society [57]

Horizontal relationship

The great contribution of Protestants to the development of society was the recognition of the equality of human rights and freedoms for all regardless of gender, race, nationality, language, origin, property and official status, place of residence, attitude to religion, beliefs, membership in public associations, etc. These relations based on equality called in modern language - horizontal.

Lack of restrictions allows each person to realize their abilities. This permits rapid progress in countries with horizontal relations.

Vertical relationship

These relations were widespread in the era of feudalism, when power was moving vertically: the feudal lord was the suzerain of his vassal — the peasant, but he himself was a vassal of the prince or king. In this way the vertical lined up.

Such relations have survived to our time in some eastern countries, although not in such a pure form as during feudalism.

Eastern philosophers preached obedience.

Lao Tzu said: "The path can only be found in humility, in the calm acceptance of life and things as they are, and in the search for an understanding of the passage of time and the development of nature."

Confucius preached three foundations (the absolute power of the sovereign over the subjects, the father over the son, the husband over the wife).

Buddha preached moral improvement, recognizing that human life is suffering. He urged to give up desires that lead to suffering, but not to a change the external way of life.

Orthodox church taught to fulfill the will of the superiors and seek the personal salvation through prayers and rituals.

As a consequence of this way of reasoning was born the Eastern vertical. A vertical society is usually very stable. The development of society is slow due to many restrictions.

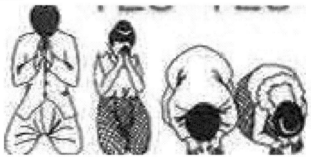

In this figure, four people are standing in front of one more powerful person. The first pair must have a higher position in society, so they are inclined less than the second pair.

In the following picture, the girl is tilted in different ways, presumably in front of three people occupying a different place in the vertical (from left to right - from the strong to the stronger and to the strongest).

Once in Thailand, I was at the birthday of a rich and powerful person. It was a very lush festivity with mountains of food, a multitude of flowers and even fireworks. When it came time to congratulate the birthday man, he sat down in a large armchair, and the youth of his huge family lined up in a long row on their knees. Then they walked one by one on their knees, kissed his hand, spoke congratulations and went far away on their knees to make room for the next, and then got up.

The relations in the Thai society can be seen on the pictures of King's Vajiralongkorn marriage with his security chief Suthida.[58]

Since the last century, democracy began to spread throughout Asia. Horizontal relations have been accepted in most Asian countries, but changes are being introduced slowly. The ruling classes are in no hurry to abandon vertical relations, because the vertical creates stability in the country, since every person must know his place in the line.

An American professor who worked for four years in Japan told me that one had to be born in Japan in order to know to whom you should bend from what angle. The system is very complex, it depends on the relationship of the two participants, and it must be absorbed with mother's milk.

At one time I worked at the university in Thailand. Greeting in Thailand is called Wai. Wai is done like this: standing upright, fold your arms in front of your face and tilt your head. This way equals greet each other, for example, two professors. If there is a person who is at a lower level in society, then he makes Wai, and the stronger person responds with a nod. The student does Wai, and the professor nods slightly. I welcomed everyone with Wai: professors, students and workers, although I knew the rule.

In the morning, when I went to my office, there was usually a cleaning woman who washed the floors. The cleaning woman got scared when I did the Wai. After the second time, the cleaning woman seeing me from far away, rushed to her knees, turned her back and rubbed the floor, pretending that she did not see me. She did not want me to do Wai, since she did not think that we were equal. It would be a violation of the rules she was taught.

In all Asian states were adopted Constitutions recognizing equality of their citizens before the law. But in reality such equality is hard to achieve in the vertical society.

Only in a horizontal society, the Constitution does work. The constitution and vertical power are mutually exclusive concepts.

ACKNOWLEDGEMENTS

I am highly indebted to my Bible teacher Rev. Dr. Carl Schenck of Missouri United Methodist Church. His lessons and discussions were deep, thorough, and very interesting.

I would like to express my deep gratitude to the editor Diane Peterson for her editorial help, valuable discussions and encouragement.

I highly appreciate critical reading of the book and profound observations made by Nadia Brunstein and Vitaly Shapovalov.

I express my warm thanks for all my friends for their ongoing support and encouragement.

REFERENCES

Part I

PRE-CHRISTIAN RELIGIONS

1. Paganism

1. Владимир Даль - О поверьях, суевериях и предрассудках   русского народа.
http://royallib.com/book/ivanovich_dal/o_poveryah_s ueveriyah_i_predrassudkah_russkogo_naroda.html

2.   Sumer civilization

1.   Sumer
https://www.history.com/topics/ancient-middle-east/sumer
2.   Sumer
https://www.ancient.eu/sumer/
3   The Code of Ur-Nammu & Legacy
https://www.ancient.eu/Ur-Nammu/
4.   The Code of Hammurabi
http://avalon.law.yale.edu/ancient/hamframe.asp

3. Civilization of ancient Egypt

1. Book of the Dead,
   https://en.wikipedia.org/wiki/Book_of_the_Dead
   The Egyptian Afterlife & The Feather of Truth
   https://www.ancient.eu/article/42/the-egyptian-
   afterlife--the-feather- of-truth/

4. Judaism

1. Ernest Badge, The book of the dead
   http://www.sacred-texts.com/egy/ebod/index.htm

5. East Asia Religions

1. Lao Tzu, Tao Te Ching
   https://www.goodreads.com/work/quotes/100074-
   d-o-d-j-ng
2. Heraclitus | Internet Encyclopedia of Philosophy
   https://www.iep.utm.edu/heraclit/
3. Confucius quotes
   https://www.brainyquote.com/authors/confucius
4. Buddhism
   http://www.bbc.co.uk/religion/religions/buddhism/
5. Despotism
   https://en.wikipedia.org/wiki/Despotism

6. Zoroastrianism

1. Zarathustra
   https://www.britannica.com/biography/Zarathustra
2. Zoroastrianism,
   http://www.bbc.co.uk/religion/religions/zoroastrian/
3. Avesta
   http://www.avesta.org/
4. Persian Empire
   https://www.history.com/topics/ancient-middle-east/persian-empire
5. The Royal Road
   https://en.wikipedia.org/wiki/Royal_Road

Part II

CRISTIANITY

The New Oxford Annotated Bible, New York, Oxford University Press
The Bible, New International Version (NIV)
The references in the Russian language can be read with Google Translate

1. First seven ecumenical councils,
   https://en.wikipedia.org/wiki/First_seven_Ecumenical_Councils

2. History of the Orthodox Church,
    https://en.wikipedia.org/wiki/History_of_the_Orthodox
    Church
3. Eastern Christianity,
    https://en.wikipedia.org/wiki/Eastern_Christianity
4. Номоканóн,
    https://ru.wikipedia.org/wiki/nomokanon
5. Saints Cyril and Methodius,
    https://www.britannica.com/biography/Saints-Cyril
    and-Methodius
    https://www.youtube.com/watch?v=wo49zWpWkz4
6. Reformation
    https://www.britannica.com/event/Reformation
7. Мартин Лютер, "95 тезисов"
    https://www.luther.de/en/95thesen.html
8. German Peasants War (1524 – 1525): Uprising of the
    Poor
    https://www.thoughtco.com/german-peasants-war-
    4150166
9. Summary of the twelve articles of the
    peasants *in* Swabia,
    https://www.unidue.de/collcart/es/sem/s6/txt07_8.html
10. List of the largest Protestant denominations
    https://en.wikipedia.org/wiki/List_of_the_largest_Prote
    stant_denominations
11. The Religious Society of Friends,

http://quaker.org/

12. Amish,
https://www.britannica.com/topic/Amish

13. Religious Landscape Study,
http://www.pewforum.org/religious-landscape-
study/importance-of- religion-in-ones- life/

14. Mount Athos
https://www.christian-pilgrimage-
journeys.com/mount- athos/4thcentury-14thcentury/
https://whc.unesco.org/en/list/454

15. About Mount Athos on "60 Minutes" American
station CBS
https://www.youtube.com/watch?v=6JTK_mOkN60

16. The Hitler Icon: How Mount Athos Honored
the Führer,
https://scottnevinssuicide.wordpress.com/2016/02/21/
the-hitler-icon-how-mountathos-honored-the-fuhrer/

17. Mount Athos: Failing Light, Monday, April 28, 1941,
TIME Magazine

18. Greece: Flight from Mt. Athos, Monday, July 13
1942. TIME Magazine

19. Third Rome Rising: The Ideologues Calling for a
New Russian Empire
https://nationalinterest.org/feature/third-rome- 16748

20. Russian Orthodox Church,
    https://www.britannica.com/topic/Russian- Orthodox-
    church

21. The enactments of Justinian. The novels - VI
    https://droitromain.univ-grenoble
    alpes.fr/Anglica/N6_Scott.htm

22. Novgorod Republic,
    https://en.wikipedia.org/wiki/Novgorod_Republic

23. Raskol, https://en.wikipedia.org/wiki/Raskol

24. Solovetsky Monastery uprising
    https://en.wikipedia.org/wiki/Solovetsky_Monastery
    _uprising

25. Giles Fletcher, Of the Russe Commonwealth

26. Нравы и быт русского народа. Извлечение
    книги Олеария "Описание путешествие в Московию"
    http://historydoc.edu.ru/catalog.asp? 52
    ob_no=12753&cat_ob_no=1

    https://www.amazon.com/Russe-Commonwealth-
    1591- Giles- Fletcher /dp/0674334159

27. Adam Olearius,
    https://en.wikipedia.org/wiki/Adam_Olearius

28. Русское Православие XVII в. глазами
    иностранных   путешественников,
    http://www.rummuseum.info/node/2599

29. Иоганн Георг Корб,   htt
    p://www.vostlit.info/Texts/rus13/Korb/pred.phtml?id
    =735

31. Корб И.Г. Дневник путешествия в Московское
    государство,1698г
    https://www.sedmitza.ru/lib/text/439160

32. В.О. Ключевский, Курс русской истории, лекции
    59-69,
    http://www.kulichki.com/inkwell/text/special/history/
    kluch/kluchlec.htm

33. Костомаров Н И - Русская история в жиз
    неописаниях ее главнейших деятелей (Отдел 1-2)
    - Страница 515-516,
    http://xwap.me/books/3012/Russkaya-istoriya-v
    zhizneopisaniyakh-yeye-glavneyshikh-deyateley-
    Otdel-12.html?p=515

34. Общественные, философские и
    политические идеи России в XIX веке,
    http://galinapop-russia.blogspot.com/2011/12/xix-
    e.html

35. Русские переводы Библии,
    http://www.primavista.ru/rus/catalog/perevod_biblii

36. Кюстин Астольф - Россия в 1839 году
    http://royallib.com/book/kyustin_astolf/rossiya_v_18
    39_godu.html

37. La Russie en 1839, Volume I by marquis de AstolpheCustine, Https://www.gutenberg.org/ebooks/25755

38. П. Я. Чаадаев Философические письма http://anthropology.rchgi.spb.ru/chaadaev/chaadaev_s1.htm

    Peter Chaadaev, Philosophical Letters & Apology of a Madman

    https://www.amazon.com/Philosophical-Letters-Apology-Yakovlevich-Chaadayev/dp/0870491024

39. Освобождение крестьян и участие в этом акте митрополита Филарета, http://mirrors.rusbible.ru/pagez.ru/philaret/about048_5.php.html

40. О шестой заповеди, http://predanie.ru/filaret-drozdov-mitropolit-moskovskiy-svyatitel/audio/153545-o-shestoy-zapovedi/

41. Толстой Лев – Исповедь http://royallib.com/book/tolstoy_lev/ispoved.html

42. О шестой заповеди, http://predanie.ru/filaretdrozdov- mitropolit-moskovskiy- svyatitel/audio/153545-o- shestoy-zapovedi/

43. Толстой Лев – Исповедь http://royallib.com/book/tolstoy_lev/ispoved.html

42. Толстой Лев - В чем моя вера,
   http://royallib.com/book/tolstoy_lev/v_chem_moya
   _vera.html

43. Переписка Толстого с Ганди,
   http://vegjournal.ru/filosofiya/tochka-zreniya/586-
   makhatma-   gandi-i-lev- tolstoy-istoriya
   perepiski.html

44. Декрет II Всероссийского съезда Советов о земле
   http://www.hist.msu.ru/ER/Etext/DEKRET/o_zemle.
   html

45. Декре́т об отделе́нии це́ркви от госуда́рства и
   шко́лы от це́ркви
   http://constitution.garant.ru/history/act1600-
   1918/5325/

46. Святитель Тихон (1865–1925), Патриарх
   Московский и Всея России, http://martyr-
   spb.ru/martyr/1475

47. Священномученик Петр (Полянский):
   недипломатичный архиерей,
   http://www.pravmir.ru/svyashhennomuchenik- petr-
   polyanskij-nediplomatichnyj-arxierej/

48. Сергий (в миру Страгородский Иван Николаевич),
   http://www.hrono.ru/biograf/bio_s/sergi_starogor.php

49. Патриа́рх Алекси́й II (в миру — Алексе́й
   Миха́йлович Ри́дигер, https://ru.wikipedia.org/wiki/
   Алекси́й II

http://news.bbc.co.uk/2/hi/europe/7767015.stm

50. Кирилл (патриарх Московский)
http://www.uznayvse.ru/znamenitosti/biografiya-patriarh- kirill.html
https://ru.wikipedia.org/wiki/Кирилл_(патриарх_Мо сковский)

51. Лето патриарха: яхта за €600 000 и воздержание от протестов,
http://www.currenttime.tv/a/27264688.html
https://ok.ru/freedomnewsprivolzsky/topic/64365087 902552

52. Свой миллиардный капитал Патриарх Кирилл (Гундяев) «сколотил» в лихие 90-е
http://uainfo.org/blognews/11873-svoy-milliardnyy-kapital-patriarh-irill-gundyaev-skolotil-v-lihie-90-

53. Патриарх Кирилл призвал бороться против защиты прав человека
http://ru.tsn.ua/svit/patriarh-kirill-prizval-borotsya-protiv-zaschity-prav-cheloveka-599461.html

54. Патриарх Московский и всея Руси Кирилл назвал борьбу с террористами на Ближнем   Востоке священной войной
http://www.interfax.by/news/world/1205734

55. Всеволод Чаплин,
https://charter97.org/ru/news/2015/6/19/156188/

56. A. Kuraev. Temptation that come from "right

A. Кураев. Искушение, которое, приходит «справа»

https://predanie.ru/book/187425-iskushenie-kotoroe-
prihodit-sprava/

57. Horizontal and vertical relationships in society
https://terminclature.wordpress.com/2013/09/20/verti
cal-vs-horizontal-relationships/

58. King Vajiralongkorn of Thailand marries his security
chief Suthida, makes her queen
https://www.cbsnews.com/news/vajiralongkorn-king-
thailand-marries-queen-suthida-former-security-
chief-today-2019-05-02/

Made in the USA
Lexington, KY
12 November 2019